Self Confidence for Tweens

5 CONFIDENCE TOOLS TO BUILD SELF IMAGE, IMPROVE SOCIAL SKILLS, BECOME BRAVE & STRONGER AND FIND YOUR OWN UNIQUE STYLE

MARTA NEGRÓN

© **Copyright Marta Negrón 2023 - All rights reserved.**

The content contained within this book may not be reproduced, duplicated, or transmitted without direct written permission from the author or the publisher.

Under no circumstances will any blame or legal responsibility be held against the publisher, or author, for any damages, reparation, or monetary loss due to the information contained within this book. Either directly or indirectly. You are responsible for your own choices, actions, and results.

Legal Notice:

This book is copyright protected. This book is only for personal use. You cannot amend, distribute, sell, use, quote, or paraphrase any part of the content within this book without the consent of the author or publisher.

Disclaimer Notice:

Please note that the information contained within this document is for educational and entertainment purposes only. All effort has been executed to present accurate, up-to-date, reliable, and complete information. No warranties of any kind are declared or implied. Readers acknowledge that the author is not engaging in the rendering of legal, financial, medical, or professional advice. The content within this book has been derived from various sources. Please consult a licensed professional before attempting any techniques outlined in this book.

By reading this document, the reader agrees that under no circumstances is the author responsible for any losses, direct or indirect, which are incurred as a result of the use of the information contained within this document, including, but not limited to — errors, omissions, or inaccuracies.

Contents

Introduction	V
1. I Am Going to Be (name of your dream)	1
2. Be Uncomfortable and Gain Confidence	11
3. Believe in Yourself, Girl	25
4. The Secret Tool: Creativity	39
5. From Boring to Stylish	51
6. How to Make a Fashion Mood Board & Develop Your Style	63
7. Practice Confidence	79
8. Social Confidence	91
9. The Secret Language That Affects Our Confidence	109
10. Compassion in Action	121
Conclusion	131
References	137

Introduction

HELLO, MY DEAR FRIEND!

CONFIDENCE IS LIKE WEARING your favorite outfit and feeling magnificent in it! You look in the mirror and admire everything about what you're wearing. The colors, the style, how it fits, and most importantly, how it makes you feel. You're sure you can walk into any room and light it up because you're glowing. At that moment, you think you can become that girl you imagine yourself being. But you don't have that feeling when you take the outfit off. I've got some good news for you; I'm going to teach you how to always be confident! With the secrets I will give you, you'll feel like you're always wearing your favorite clothes. But instead of clothes, you will be wearing your confidence outfit.

Let me introduce myself, my name is Marta Negron, and I wrote this book because I worked as a fashion designer for 27 years and there was one thing I noticed about the o did fashion shows. The creative ones had a lot of confidence. Wow! Apparently, creative kids have higher levels of confidence. Fascinating! One girl, in particular, became very dear to my heart because she stood out like a bright and shining star, her name was Leonora, and you'll meet her in chapter one. I want you to meet her because I want her to help me teach you how to be confident. Trust me when I tell you she is really amazing.

What impressed me about Leonora is that she hasn't always been confident. Like a lot of you girls reading this, she struggled to fit in with her friends and felt like she needed to dress and act in a certain way so that the kids in her school would like her; she didn't make eye contact when meeting new kids, and she didn't like trying new things in case she wasn't good at them. But life got really fun for Leonora when she realized how creative she was and found her own style.

So, I've teamed up with Leonora to write this book, and I want to give you a little sneak peek at the things you can expect to learn:

- Learn the five powerful confidence tools.
- How to develop and rock your own unique style.
- How to unleash your creativity and become sensational.
- How to stay true to yourself when your friends are following the crowd.

- How to become confident doing things you're not comfortable with.

- The importance of having the right friends who will encourage and motivate you.

Develop the confidence that makes you fearless to become the spectacular girl you were born to be. I want you to work at achieving your biggest dreams with complete confidence that you'll turn them into a reality. Don't worry; you're not doing this alone; I'll be your guiding light like a big sister helping you navigate the challenges of becoming a teenager. So, if you're ready to start your confidence journey, give me a virtual high-five! Let's go and become the best tween version of yourself.

Chapter 1

1

I Am Going to Be (name of your dream)

"Confidence begins in your heart, and it's up to you to let it shine."
~ Leonora

Hey, it's really cool to meet you. I'm Leonora; I love meeting friendly, kind, and fabulous girls like yourself. I'm 11 years old and like many things, but my favorite thing is using my sketchbook to draw some of my fashion ideas. My mom, Anna, is an artisan, and she tells me that fashion is an art form that encourages creativity and boosts your confidence. Before, I was not too confident, but I learned to create my unique fashion style by using creativity and fashion. Knowing that I look good and feel good in my own style boosts my confidence. My mom is right. Let your creativity shine!

I will tell you I love wearing ankle boots, and my favorite clothes are a fake black leather jacket and a t-shirt with my favorite bands on the front. But I also like mixing it up too. Or if I'm feeling a bit more hip, I'll mix the rock and the hip-hop look. The hip-hop pants are so comfortable, and they look great with my leather jacket or any jacket.

But what I love the most is helping friends like you find cool outfits you can feel confident and comfortable in. My dream is to start my own clothing line one day. I will call it 'Reina Mora,' and I really can't wait until it happens; it will be totally magical. You might be thinking, "You sound like you've got a lot of clothes, and I don't have that many clothes." You don't need too many clothes to express yourself and look stylish.

I go shopping with my mom to buy some of my clothes with the money I save from walking dogs in my neighborhood, helping my classmates with their Spanish assignments, and helping around the house by doing things like loading the dishwasher, folding laundry, setting the table, and sometimes washing the cars with my father or mother on the weekends. And you don't need to buy expensive clothes either, some of my favorite items are as cheap as $5! Isn't that cool?

I know I am only 11 years old (I'll be 12 very soon), but I can teach you everything I've learned and know about fashion. You will see me throughout the book wearing nine fashion styles. I know a little about fashion. The more I learn about styles, the more confident I feel because I can be and express myself better.

I AM GOING TO BE (NAME OF YOUR DREAM)   3

The girl that uses Self Confidence as her best outfit

Rock Style

Oh, and by the way, I wrote the quote at the beginning just for you because it's how I started my confidence journey.

I made the decision to be confident in my heart first, and then I practiced so that I believed it and everyone else saw it. The tennis player Sloane Stephens said, "When you have confidence, you can do anything." Trust me when I tell you that it's true. When I didn't have confidence, there was no way I could have walked on a fashion show runway in front of 600 people! And that's why I want you to have confidence so you can do anything too! That's all I've got to say right now; I'll see you again soon. Oh, I almost forgot you will also meet my super cute dog. His name is Rocco.

Yes! I want you to think about some of the things you would do if you were fearless in doing them. Use your wildest imagination and dream as far as your dreams will take you. Now write them down on a piece of paper like this: "I AM GOING TO BE [name of your dream]." You can write down as many things as you want. Next, I want you to fold that paper and put it under your pillow. When you wake up in the morning, read it out loud, and do the same before you go to sleep at night. Let me tell you why you should do this.

There is a famous comedian on TV called Steve Harvey; a comedian tells a lot of jokes and makes people laugh.

When he was about nine years old, his swimming coach told everyone to stand up and say to their classmates what they wanted to become when they grew up. Steve went to the front of the class and in a big brave voice told everyone that he wanted to be a comedian and be on TV. His swimming coach did not believe in dreams, and he told him to stop being silly and come up with something that he would really be able to do.

Steve said that was what he wanted to do, and he didn't listen to his swimming coach. Well, his swimming coach got mad and reported him to his parents. But his parents agreed with Steve and told him he could be whoever he wanted to be if he was prepared to work hard at it. So his dad told him to write his dream down on a piece of paper and read it out loud when he woke up in the morning and when he went to bed at night. And so that's exactly what Steve did.

Guess what? Today, Steve Harvey is all grown up, and he's one of the most successful comedians in the world, and his shows are on TV everywhere! Should I tell you what his secret was? He had confidence. Do you want to know what confidence means? Keep reading.

♥ ♥ ♥ ♥ ♥

What is Confidence?

Confidence means that you believe in yourself. You know what you're good at, and you trust that you can learn something new if you want to. But confidence also means accepting that you're not good at everything. For example, you might know you play a musical instrument well. When the teacher calls you to the front of the class to play the song you've been practicing, you stand up with pride and play because you know you can do it.

On the other hand, you might realize that you're not a very good singer, but your friend is. You're not jealous of her because that's what she's good at, and you're good at playing a musical instrument. You both have your unique gifts, you're happy for her, and she's happy for you. Confidence also means accepting yourself for who you are and what you look like.

What Confidence Isn't

There are some things that you might think are confidence, but they are not. I'll tell you what they are:

Being Unkind: Do you have any bullies in your school? They walk around like they own the school. They sit at the back of the classroom and cause a lot of distractions, and sometimes the teacher has to throw them out because they're making things difficult for everyone else. They call children names, and sometimes, they even hit them. Most kids are scared of bullies because of the things they do. Well, I've got some good news for you, being unkind doesn't make you confident. The truth is it means you don't have any confidence. When kids are unkind, it means they feel bad about themselves. You should actually feel sorry for bullies. Sometimes, they act that way because they have been bullied before, and the only way they can deal with it is by bullying other kids.

Being Loud: There's absolutely nothing wrong with being loud, some people have louder voices than others, and that's okay. But some people are loud on purpose because they want to be the center of attention. They want everyone to focus on them, and if someone else gets more attention than them, they'll get even louder. Wanting all eyes on you isn't confidence; it's attention-seeking.

Showing Off: A show-off is someone who believes they are better than everyone else because of what they own. So anytime they get something new, they run around telling everyone about it. But they're not doing it because they're excited; they want to make everyone jealous. It's wonderful to tell your friends your good news but tell them for the right reasons.

Being Outgoing: Have you ever met anyone who always seems lively? They're the life of all the parties, and everyone wants to be around them because they've got such good vibes. Having an outgoing personality is an excellent quality, but it doesn't mean you're confident. Some outgoing people don't have confidence, but having an outgoing personality becomes even more attractive when they do have confidence.

♥ ♥ ♥ ♥ ♥

Why Is It Important to Have Confidence?

After reading about what confidence is, I'm sure you think it's great. Do you want to be confident? If you're alone right now, shout out, "YES! I WANT TO BE CONFIDENT!" Confidence is fantastic, there are many reasons why, and I will tell you what they are.

You Won't Give Up: When you know you're good at something and were born to do it, you will never give up. Do you remember what I told you about Steve Harvey? It wasn't easy for him to become a comedian; a lot of people said that he wasn't good enough and they wouldn't give him a job. But he kept trying, and eventually, someone gave him a chance, which was how he became famous. Sometimes you will find obstacles and challenges that make your dream a little difficult. Remember, do not give up. Always remember your dreams.

You Will Have Less Fear: Do you sometimes think, "I can't do it," or "That's too hard for me?" Don't worry; everyone feels like that, even people who are really confident. The difference between the people who are confident and those who are not is that confident people speak to themselves with their inner magical voice. When they get worried and start saying things like, "You can't do it," their magical voice says, "Yes, I can do it," and then they'll go ahead and do it even if they are still a bit scared. You've got this magical voice, too; you've just got to use it.

Better Relationships: Do you want to have better relationships with your loved ones? Confidence will help you achieve this because when you're confident, you stop thinking about your insecurities, and you can enjoy the company of others. When you're not sure, you do things like avoid people, and acting like this can make it hard for your friends to want to be around you.

Do you feel you have a better understanding of confidence?

Let me give you a quick reminder:

- Confidence is believing in yourself and accepting yourself.

- Confidence isn't about being unkind, loud, showing off, or being outgoing.

- It's essential to have confidence because it means you won't give up.

- You will have less fear, you'll feel strong, and you'll have better relationships.

In chapter two, you'll learn all about the first confidence tool in your confidence tool kit. I will talk about how you can improve your confidence by doing the things that don't make you feel so good. You'll be amazed at how much those things you don't like can make your life so much better.

Chapter 2

2

Be Uncomfortable and Gain Confidence

"Uncomfortable does not mean bad, uncomfortable means you are doing something you have not done before." ~ Joe Vita

HI FRIEND, IN THIS book, you'll learn about five special tools that will help you gain confidence. The first tool is all about getting out of your comfort zone, it's really exciting, and together, we're going to talk about it in this chapter. Are you ready to learn about the first special tool to help you get confidence? Excellent, here it goes...

To Be Confident You Have to be Uncomfortable

Okay, so you remember I just said that the first special tool is about getting out of your comfort zone. In case you're not sure what that means, let me help you understand it a bit better. So being uncomfortable basically means you're not comfortable. That sounds really simple, doesn't it? But let me help you out a bit more. Let's say you're in class, and a teacher asks a question expecting someone to answer it; you don't know the answer, so you don't put your hand up. But the teacher calls your name and asks you to answer the question.

As soon as you hear your name, you start feeling a bit scared because you don't know the answer. But because your teacher can see you're unsure, she tries to help you by giving you some ideas about what the answer could be. In the beginning, you felt a bit scared because you didn't know the answer at all, but you started feeling a bit better because now you have a few clues about what the answer might be. You say one thing, and it's not the correct answer, so the teacher keeps giving you clues until you get it right. The closer you get to the right answer, the more confident you get. That's sort of what it feels like to be uncomfortable. Does that make sense? I'll let Leonora tell you more about how being uncomfortable makes you confident.

Hey, it's Leonora. Like Marta said, being uncomfortable will help you to become more confident. Let me tell you a story. So, a little while after finding my favorite style, my mom and I went shopping, and I was wearing a really cool outfit. I felt really confident because I loved what I was wearing. A denim jacket with some embroidery, patterned leggings, a t-shirt, and ankle boots. That was the day I met Marta; she came up to my mom and said hi, introduced herself, and asked my mom if I was her daughter. She said I looked great and she'd like me to take part in her fashion show. I said yes right away, but my mom said she'd check it out, and Marta went on her way. To cut a long story short, my mom checked her out, and I ended up going to the fashion show.

That day was so awesome, but I was nervous at the same time because I'd never done a fashion show. I was very UNCOMFORTABLE! When I arrived and saw all the people, I got even more nervous; my stomach was doing backflips! But deep down, I knew I could do it. Marta was the designer of the fashion show, and she was the one who told me it was okay to be nervous. That it was normal because it was my first time doing a fashion show. She told me, "Leonora, when you walk the runway, think of something you love to do. Just concentrate on that and keep walking. You can do it." I still felt uncomfortable, and then it was my turn on the runway for my first fashion show. I walked down that runway and started imagining I was riding my bike. But then, like a miracle, everyone started cheering for me, and I could see my mom and friends in the audience clapping; I felt like I could do anything! After the fashion show, I had more confidence than ever. And that's how I want you to feel when you start trying new things. First, you will feel uncomfortable, it happened to me, but you have to do it. Try it!!

Trying Something New Sounds Scary, But It Works

Leonora's story was really inspiring, wasn't it? Now I want to talk to you about trying something new. There are a lot of famous people who were scared when they first got started as children. Do you know who Emma Watson is? She's the young actress who played the part of Hermoine Granger in Harry Potter. She's a fantastic actress, right? You'd never think she was scared of being in front of the cameras, would you? But she was. Emma was only nine years old when she played Hermoine Granger, and she said she was really scared on her first day. She'd never been in such a big film before, and it made her worry a bit. But once she got used to her new job, she really enjoyed it, and she became a lot more confident.

Have you heard of Wolfgang Amadeus Mozart? (Let's call him Mozart.) Maybe not because he was alive a long time ago. But he was really famous for making music, and when he was only six years old, he played the piano for a really important person. And guess what? Mozart was really scared because the person he was playing for was a special lady, and he wanted to make sure he got it right. Even though Mozart was really scared, he played the piano anyway, and she was really impressed. When Mozart grew up, he became really famous for the music he made.

Do you like football? Because the last person I want to talk about is a football player called Lionel Messi. He was much younger than the two people you've just read about because he started playing football when he was only four years old! Isn't that amazing? Lionel began to play for his local football club. But because he was smaller than his other teammates, he was afraid he wouldn't be good enough. Well, he was good enough, and when he grew up, he became a very successful football player.

BE UNCOMFORTABLE AND GAIN CONFIDENCE 15

The girl that keeps a journal of her own experiences

Girly Style

All of these famous people I've mentioned were just like you when they first got started. But because they went ahead and did it anyway, all became very good at what they were doing, and today, they are known all over the world. Do you want to be good at something? If you do, you'll have to do what these people did.

♥ ♥ ♥ ♥ ♥

You Will Feel a Little Nervous, But It Is Normal

Wouldn't it be great if we could be good at everything without feeling nervous when we want to try something new? I know I'd like that, but unfortunately, life doesn't work like that. The good news is that it's totally normal to feel this way; let me explain.

Our brains work in a certain way, and it likes to do things that it knows how to do because that's how we feel safe. When we try something new and we're not used to it, our brains get a bit confused because it doesn't know what's going to happen, and that's when we start feeling nervous. But here's the thing, when we try something new, we're also learning and growing.

It's important to remember that if you don't feel good about feeling nervous when you're trying something new, it's okay because everyone feels like this, even adults. It's a normal feeling, and there are plenty of people who think exactly the same way, so don't worry, okay?

So if you're feeling nervous about trying something new, don't get too worried about it. Please take a few deep breaths and remember that it's normal to feel this way. Instead, focus on the excitement of learning something new and how cool it will be when you finally get the hang of it.

You Get to Learn so Much From Trying New Things

Learning new things is a fun and exciting experience because it helps us grow. Whether you're learning a sport or a new subject at school, you learn new skills you didn't know anything about before. For example, the first time you cook, you might decide that you really like it and can't wait to do it again. But trying something new also teaches you what you don't like. You might try painting for the first time and decide that it's not for you and that you don't want to paint again.

So the next time you try something new, remember that it's a fun opportunity for you to grow and learn. You never know what new and exciting things could be waiting for you to try.

It Doesn't Matter if You Don't Succeed on the First Try

Think about it like a baby learning to walk. They don't start walking straight away, do they? They fall down a lot, but every time they get up and try again, they're learning how to take steps and how to balance. This is what happens to you when you try something new.

You're never going to be perfect at the new thing you're trying because it takes practice and time to get better. Let me ask you a question. Can you swim or ride a bike? If yes, think about when you were learning how to do it. You probably went under the water a couple of times or fell off your bike, right? But after some practice, you learned how to do it, right? The same happens when you try new things like playing a musical instrument, sports, or art. You won't get it right the first time, but that's okay.

Also, getting stuff wrong is really important because that's how you learn. When you make a mistake, you can learn from it and figure out how to do it better next time. Do you do puzzles? If so, what happens when you put a piece in the wrong spot? You take it out, look for another piece, and try again, right? You'll try again, and you'll keep trying. Trying new things works in the same way. If we don't get it right the first time, we just learn from our mistakes and try again.

The last thing I want to say is that success isn't always about getting it right the first time. It is about doing the best you can and learning from your experiences. Even famous inventors didn't get it right the first time, and you know people who make things are really clever, right? Do you know who Thomas Edison is? He created a light bulb, but he didn't get it right the first time. Guess how many times it took for him to do it? Are you ready for this? It took him 1,000 attempts! That's a lot. And I'm sure most people would have given up a lot sooner, but Thomas Edison did not, so he kept trying. Do you really want to succeed? If so, you'll need to keep trying like Thomas Edison.

Walking Through Your Fear and Doing Things Anyway

Have you ever felt scared when you were trying something new? I've already mentioned that it's normal to feel nervous, but fear is a bit different, isn't it? When you're nervous, you just feel a bit funny on the inside, but when you're afraid, you might start shaking or even crying because you think you might get it wrong. But it's important to remember to walk through your fear and do it anyway. Why is that? Because that's what makes you strong. I remember many years ago when I was little; I was scared to go to sleep with the light off. But one day, even though I was still afraid, I felt brave enough to turn the light off. I was really happy and slept every night with the light off after that.

You've got to do the same; you might be scared to try something new, but once you do it, you'll realize it wasn't that bad after all, and you'll have more confidence because you decided to do it anyway, even though you were scared.

Just Gaining Confidence

The whole idea of being uncomfortable is to gain confidence. That's what you want, right? Good, because one way to get it is to do things you're not that good at, and the better you become at it, the more your confidence will grow. You see, confidence is like a muscle; the more you use it, the more it grows and the stronger it gets. So the next time you're trying something new and feel uncomfortable, remember it's actually a good thing. It means you're pushing yourself to grow and learn. Find a way to like the discomfort, and you'll be surprised at what you can achieve.

Start With Little Things That Make You Curious

As you've read, trying something new can make you nervous and scared. That's why it's important to start with the small things when trying something new, so you don't get too nervous and scared. Think about it like this; if you couldn't swim, you wouldn't jump in at the deep end, would you? That wouldn't be a very good idea because you can't swim. So, what would you do instead? You'd go to the pool's shallow end first and might even put on some floats to be extra safe, right? Well, that's what you should do when you're trying something new, start with the small stuff first.

Do you remember reading about how the brain works when we try something new? If not, let me remind you. It feels a bit uncomfortable because it's not used to doing the new thing. But when you start small, it's not so much of a surprise. For example, you might have an interest in fashion and want to enter a fashion show. But you're a bit nervous about walking around in front of so many people. A smaller version of this might be to do a fashion parade for your family first, and then you can do one with your friends. When you've done enough fashion parades for your friends and family, you'll have enough confidence to enter a real show. Sounds like a good idea, right?

Starting small is how you develop confidence because when something's too hard, you might get upset with getting it wrong all the time, and you won't want to try anymore. But because it's not too hard, you'll feel better about trying again, and the more you get it right, the more confidence you will get.

Can I ask you one last question in this chapter? What are some of the things you're curious about? You know, stuff you've never tried before, but you want to know about it. It could be anything, even trying food or drink you've never tasted before. I want you to get a pen and paper and write a list of everything you're curious about, from the small things to the big things. When you're ready, I want you to start trying out these new things starting with the smallest first. It will be really fun to work your way through the list and cross each thing off that you try, right? I can't wait until you get started with this, and remember, whenever you decide to get started, I'll be cheering you on.

So there you have it! Starting small is important when trying something new because it makes things easier to learn and helps you become more confident.

Some Words to Make You Brave

You've read all about feeling nervous and scared when trying something new. I understand that you don't want to feel anxious or scared, so I'm going to give you something that will make things a bit easier for you. What I'm going to give you are some words, and they're not just any words, by the way; they're unique words that will make you feel brave before you start something new. What you've got to do is say these words just before you're about to do something new. I want you to repeat them over and over again until you feel strong and ready to go. So you'll need to take this book with you when you're going to do something new, so you'll have your special words ready.

Here are the unique words I want you to say:

- I believe in myself
- Trying something new is exciting and fun

- I don't mind making mistakes because every mistake I make will help me learn and grow

- It's okay to start small and take your time because that's how you make progress

- I won't compare myself to anyone; I am special in my own way

- Even when it's hard, don't give up because you'll be really proud of yourself

- I am supported by my family and friends

Remember, we all need a little encouragement sometimes, it's great when other people encourage you, but it's even better when you can cheer yourself up. And don't feel shy about speaking to yourself either because all successful people do it.

♥ ♥ ♥ ♥ ♥

After reading this, do you feel you're ready to start trying out new things and making yourself uncomfortable? I hope so. Here's a quick reminder of what you've just read:

- Being uncomfortable is the first tool in your confidence tool kit.

- The way you make yourself uncomfortable is by trying new things.

- You'll be a bit scared and nervous when you try

something new, but that's okay because it's normal to feel that way.

- You don't have to get it right the first time, and it's okay to make mistakes because that's how you grow
- You learn a lot when you try new things, including what you like and don't like.
- Walking through your fear and doing things anyway.
- Start with the small things first to get comfortable with being uncomfortable.

Say your unique words to make you brave when you feel nervous or scared.

Are you looking forward to finding out what else is in your confidence tool kit? If so, turn the page with me and keep reading!

Chapter 3

3

Believe in Yourself, Girl

"Don't waste your energy trying to change opinions...
Do your thing, and don't care if they like it." ~ Tina Fey

I'M GLAD TO SEE you've made it to the third chapter. I hope you've learned a lot so far and you're looking forward to learning more. The second confidence tool is to believe in yourself. When you believe in yourself, you feel more confident and strong. This helps you when things get a bit difficult.

You might feel a little bit nervous and even scared, but you'll do it anyway because you believe in yourself. Life gets really exciting because you know you can do it if you try. Do you remember that Leonora walked on the runway using and trying the first powerful confidence tool?

You know that you're awesome just the way you are. It means you can be your own cheerleader and push yourself when you need to. Celebrate progress no matter how small.

You feel more comfortable doing things that you wouldn't normally do when you believe in yourself. Like if your parents ask you to do something around the house that one of your older brothers or sisters usually does. When you believe in yourself, you feel more confident, and you'll take on the challenge. When your parents see how well you've done, they will be proud of you and feel confident enough to ask you to do other stuff to help around the house.

I want to take a moment to remind you how amazing you are, you can do anything you want to do in life, and there's absolutely nothing that can stop you! Be patient with yourself.

How to Gain and Discover Your Strengths and Recognize Your Weaknesses

Did you know that everyone has something they're really good at and things they're not so good at? The things that you're good at are called your strengths, and the things that you're not so good at are called your weaknesses. Some people are not happy about having weaknesses because they want to be good at everything, but it doesn't matter at all. It's nothing to be embarrassed about. Confidence comes from accepting that your strengths and weaknesses are part of being human. Let's start by talking about how to find your strengths:

What Do You Love: The things you love doing give you an idea about your strengths. You enjoy doing these things and don't need to put much effort into doing them. For example, you might love drawing, dancing, solving math problems, or writing short stories. I'll let Leonora tell you a quick story about how she found one of her strengths.

Hi guys, so when I was about eight years old, my mom, Anna, who is a fantastic artisan, started getting me to help her organize her studio, which was kind of disorganized. It was so cool going to her studio. So many colors, types of equipment, and materials. I thought her studio was the most amazing thing ever, and on some weekends, I would sort out her materials into different categories, such as brushes, paints, and tools, and label the containers. My mom was really impressed because I was saving her so much space. I learned that organizing was one of my strengths, and I felt confident. Today my mom pays me some money to help organize her materials because she doesn't like doing it! Awesome right? Here's Marta again.

Ask People: Sometimes, we don't really know what we're good at because we do them so quickly that we don't really think about them. When I was a little girl, I loved writing, and I used to write all the time. If a friend or a member of my family needed something written, they would ask me to do it. English was also my favorite subject in school, and now that I'm grown up, I write books and have learned that one of my strengths is writing. I didn't know it when I was a little girl, and that's why I want to help you learn about your strengths.

Try New Things: In chapter two, you read all about learning new things; you know that it helps you gain confidence, but learning new things also helps you find your strengths. Some of you might not know what your strengths are because you have yet to find them. There might be subjects you're good at in school, but you don't love them. They don't make you feel good inside. When you find your strength, you'll love it and want to do it all the time. When I was a little girl, I loved writing so much that when it was dinner time, my mom would have to come upstairs into my room to get me because I was so focused on my writing.

Remember, if you don't know what your strengths are, it might take a while to find them, but that doesn't matter. It's better you take your time and do things the right way. Now let's look at how you can find your weaknesses.

What Do You Find Hard: What things do you find hard and wish you didn't have to ever do? Whatever they are, they are your weaknesses. Recognizing your weaknesses gives you an opportunity to grow. It might be drawing, swimming, or playing a musical instrument. When I was in school, I found it really hard to read music, and as soon as I was old enough not to take that subject anymore, I dropped it like a hot potato! Music was definitely my weakness.

Ask People: The people closest to you will definitely know what your weaknesses are because they spend a lot of time with you, and sometimes, they know you better than you know yourself. So, if you're not sure what your weaknesses are, ask your friends and family members, and they will be able to help you.

Be Honest: Being honest with yourself helps you find your weaknesses because sometimes we try to make ourselves believe we're good at something because we think we're supposed to be good at it. For example, you might hate swimming and not be good at it. But because your sister is good at swimming and she loves it, and people are always saying nice things to her because of it, you think you should be good at swimming too, but the truth is, you don't like it. Are there things you pretend to like because you think you've got to like them? If you've answered yes to this question, this could be your weakness. Listen, it's okay not to like stuff; it's not normal to enjoy everything and be good at everything, so don't worry about it. When you admit this to yourself, you'll feel a lot better, trust me.

It's Important to Surround Yourself With People Who Think You're Awesome and Want to Be Around You

The people you hang around with are really important because they can make you feel really good about yourself or make you feel really bad about yourself. And who wants to feel bad about themselves? No one, right? So that's why you've got to be careful about the friends you choose. If you think you're awesome, your friends should think you're fantastic too. Here are a few reasons why you should surround yourself with the right people:

They Give You Confidence: This book is about getting confidence, and surrounding yourself with friends who think you're fantastic will help you become more confident.

Friends who think you're awesome will say nice things about you. When you do something they don't like, they'll tell you about it, but it won't be in the wrong way. They'll let you know about it because they want you to do better. They want you to grow and become even more awesome. When you're around people who think you're fantastic, it makes you feel good about yourself.

They Accept You: It's really important to be yourself. Sometimes, people don't like you, not because you've done something wrong but because you were not meant to be friends. Now, I'm not saying it's right not to like people, but you're not always going to like people. Sometimes, what happens when people don't like you is that you try your hardest to get them to like you, and that could include acting like someone you're not. The best way is to be yourself. When you are yourself and don't try to act like others, the right friends will come into your life. Your real friends accept you for who you are, and you don't have to act around them. You can be happy, sad, or goofy around them, and they'll always love you for who you are.

They Support You: It's so cool when you think you have a good idea or want to try something new, and your friends support you. That's what real friends do; they help you because they want you to be happy and successful.

They Make Your Life Fun: When you have friends who think you're fantastic, it makes life a lot more fun. Do you want to have fun? I'm sure you answered yes to this question because everyone wants to have fun. I most certainly do!

When your friends have good vibes, you have fun, laugh, and try new things together.

Remember, it's important to hang around with people who love you for who you are. It's okay if your friends have different personalities and don't like all the same things as you because that's not what makes a good friend. A good friend is someone who makes you feel good about yourself; they accept you for who you are. You deserve to be around people who make you happy.

Stop Comparing Yourself to Others

I hope you don't mind me asking you this question. But do you compare yourself to people? You might compare yourself to your friends, brothers, sisters, or the famous people you see on TV. It's okay to measure yourself to people because everyone does it, even adults. But just because everyone does it, it doesn't mean it's the right thing to do. Let me tell you why it's not a good idea.

It Makes You Feel Sad: It's not a good idea to compare yourself to people because it makes you feel sad. Do you agree with me that when you compare yourself to people, it makes you feel sad? Do you want to know why? Because everyone is different, and we can't all be the same. The world would be a really boring place if everyone was the same, wouldn't it? Let me ask you another question, can you compare apples and oranges? Hopefully, you said no. The reason you can't compare apples and oranges is that they're not the same; you're not the same as anyone either, and that's why you shouldn't compare yourself to other people.

Focus on the Right Things: Do you want to become more confident? Then that's what you need to focus on. When you spend time comparing yourself to other people, you won't have time to gain more confidence. So if you want to become really confident, the best thing to do is spend your time working on the things I talk about in this book, and then you won't have time to compare yourself to other people because you'll be too busy becoming awesome.

Just remember it's super important to focus on yourself, building your confidence, and on the things that make you happy instead of comparing yourself to other people. You are lovely. You don't need to change anything about yourself.

Focus on Your Abilities

Hi beautiful! Focusing on your abilities is essential because these are things you're already good at. With practice, you can become even better at them. Maybe you're really good at solving puzzles, organizing, drawing, or singing. When you spend more time practicing, your skills get even better, and one day, you can call yourself an expert.

Another reason to focus on your abilities is that it helps you do great things. Let's just say you want to become an excellent soccer player, if you focus on practicing your soccer skills, you'll get really good at it, and you might be able to play for a cool soccer team. Do me a favor; I want you to get a pen and paper and write down what you'd like to be good at.

The girl that steps out of her comfort zone and tries new things

Streetwear style

Now write down everything you need to do to become really good at it. Let's use the soccer player example again. If you want to become a great soccer player, you'll need to do things like watch videos to teach you how to kick the ball around better, play with some people who are better than you so that you're pushing yourself to get better, or you might just need to spend more time practicing. If you spend half an hour a day practicing, increase the time to one hour a day.

The last thing I want to say is that focusing on your abilities and practicing all the time makes it easier to make your dreams come true. When you take small steps, you get better and better.

Give Yourself a Little Credit – Do That Everyday

Whether you've done something great or not, every day, you should give yourself credit just for being awesome. You're a really cool girl who wants to do extraordinary things to make the world better. Don't you think that deserves a clap? I do! When you give yourself credit, you're basically saying, "Hey, I've done an excellent job; I'm proud of myself. It's important to feel proud of yourself because it helps you get more confidence. And you want to be confident, don't you?

Do this every day; remember to give yourself credit, and don't feel that you need to wait until you do something great. Give yourself credit just for being awesome. But when you do something good, give yourself a little bit of extra credit. It can be anything from helping your little brother to tie his shoelaces or getting good marks on your test. Make sure you always give yourself credit for being amazing and for the amazing things you do!

Every Perfectly Imperfect Flaw is What Makes You Unique

Have you ever heard the saying, "Nobody's perfect?" Well, that's because it's true; there isn't one perfect person on the planet. A perfect person doesn't exist; you might think all the famous people you see on television are perfect, but they're not; they're just like everyone else. But guess what? It's actually a good thing that no one is perfect.

You see, all of these little things that you might think are wrong with you are actually what makes you a beautiful person. If everyone was perfect, this world would be really boring, don't you think? We would be living in a fairy-tale world, and it would be pretty weird, wouldn't it?

Maybe you have a scar on your cheek from when you fell over. Or maybe you've got a birthmark on your knee. Sometimes when you get excited and happy, you use a different cute voice. Your classmates find it a bit strange and funny. Or you get a little bit shy when you meet new people. There's nothing wrong with any of these things, and if there's anything about yourself that you feel embarrassed about, I want to let you know that you don't have to be embarrassed about it because that's what makes you who you are.

Sometimes you might feel like you need to be perfect for people to like you, so you might try and act a bit differently to fit in. But the truth is, when you're yourself, people like you more because you are not trying to act like someone else.

So the next time you feel that you need to hide something about yourself or be a different person for people to like you, remember that you're perfect just the way you are, and your true friends will like you for the real you.

♥ ♥ ♥ ♥ ♥

Remember, You Are a Special and Talented Girl Who Has Everything It Takes to Succeed in Life

♥ ♥ ♥ ♥ ♥

It's important to remember that you're unique and talented, and you've got everything it takes to succeed. It would be best if you never gave up because one day, all your dreams are going to come true. When it happens, you'll look back at all the days when you didn't feel so good, and you'll be really proud of yourself for not giving up. So never give up!

You've read a lot of words in this chapter, and I'm really proud of you for trying so hard to become more confident. Remember, your journey is unique because you are unique. To make sure that you remember everything you've read, here is a quick reminder:

- Believe in yourself is the second tool in your confidence tool kit.

- To believe in yourself means that you know you're awesome.

- You learn what your strengths are.

- You find your weaknesses.

- It's important to surround yourself with compassionate, kind people.

- You should focus on your abilities.

- You should give yourself credit because you're fantastic.

- You're not perfect, but that's a good thing; the things you might be embarrassed about are the things that make you who you are.

Do you want to know what the third confidence tool is? Only girls who like reading will ever know the answer to that. But I think you will enjoy reading it, so you can find out what it is in the next chapter.

Chapter 4

4

The Secret Tool: Creativity

"Creativity is intelligence having fun." ~ Albert Einstein

GIRLY! BEFORE WE START here, I want to let you know that chapters four, five, and six discuss fashion. Fashion? Yes, fashion! I know you thought the book was about learning how to be confident, and you're right; that's what it's about. But remember I told you I was a fashion designer for 27 years. I've worked with hundreds of girls just like you, some of them were very confident, and some of them were not very confident. Fashion boosts your confidence because you can express yourself. Remember this, creativity and fashion communicate who you are without you saying a word. That is confidence.

As a fashion designer, I did two fashion shows a year: spring/summer and fall/winter. Some of the girls who were there to participate in the fashion show were confident. Others were not confident or a little nervous, but because they loved participating in the fashion show, they were brave enough to walk the runway. Let me tell you, walking in front of 600 or more people on your own is not that easy. It's a little uncomfortable, but if you try, it makes you a fearless person with confidence. Doing something you love at the same time as having fun is also what it means to be confident.

Doing fashion shows is how I learned about the third secret tool because I noticed that the girls like Leonora, who was confidently walking the runways at the fashion shows, were helping the girls that needed to be more confident. The confident girls had something in common, they were very creative with their outfits. They made themselves stand out by having different hairstyles, decorating their shoes with rhinestones and other colorful stones, or making their pants and tops look beautiful by drawing unique designs onto them. Or carrying pretty tote bags that their moms made out of pretty fabrics.

I talked to some moms to find out why their girls were so confident at a young age, and they all had the same answer, "My daughter loves to be creative." I immediately understood that these young girls were confident because they were having fun creating a unique fashion style that made them feel good and helped them express themselves.

There are a lot of different tools to help you gain more confidence, but I am giving you the SECRET TOOL! The third tool in your confidence tool kit is CREATIVITY. I've called it the 'secret tool' because you will only read about this in a few books. Creativity is really fun, and it will give you a massive confidence boost. So girls, if you're ready to get creative and gain more confidence, give me a virtual high five and keep reading!

What It Means to Be Creative

In case you're not too sure about what it means to be creative. It's basically about using your imagination to make something unique and new. It's like building something with Lego blocks, writing a story, drawing a picture, personalizing your scrapbook, or sewing a tote bag with your mom. You get to create something using your own ideas.

Being creative is super fun because you can express yourself the way you want to. It allows you to show the world what you think and how you feel. And sometimes, when you create something really extraordinary, you might even surprise yourself.

It's also important to mention that being creative isn't just about making nice things. It's also about being able to solve problems and come up with original ideas. For example, let's say that one of the arms of your mom's glasses fell off when she was working on the computer. She looked for the repair kit but couldn't find it. So she sat down and decided she'd go to the store and buy a new repair kit to fix the glasses so that she could continue working. But you thought about it and said, "Wait a minute, Mom, I have an idea. I think that I can repair your glasses." And you went to the kitchen, got a toothpick, stuck the toothpick where the screw would go, and then trimmed the excess with your mom's help. It was not perfect, but your mom was so happy and proud of your idea.

Another reason it's cool to be creative is that you learn things about yourself you didn't know before. When you come up with new ideas, experiment, and try new things, you might find out that you've got talents you never knew you had. Isn't that awesome?

How Creativity Can Boost Your Confidence

Creativity can help you become more confident because using your imagination to create something unique and new can make you feel really proud of yourself. It makes you more confident. Do you want to know more about why being creative makes you more confident? Okay, I'll tell you.

You Challenge Yourself: When you create something or create an idea that shows everyone your thoughts, feelings, and ideas, you feel terrific about yourself. It shows you have something special to offer the world and can create something unique. And after you've completed this fantastic idea, you get to look at it and say, "Wow! This is my creation." When you create something unique, you start thinking about other amazing things you can make, and you'll have the confidence to want to challenge yourself more because you'll know that you can do it.

Make New Friends: When you're creative, there's a chance that you can make more friends because, depending on what you're doing, you might need other kids to help you out. Sometimes, these kids are not people you know already;

they're new people you've never met before. If you like each other, they might become your new friends. Everyone wants more friends because, with more friends, you can do many different things and have a lot of fun.

But did you also know that making new friends can make you more confident? Yes, it can! Here's why. Because other kids make friends with you because they like you and want to spend more time with you. Can you guess how you feel when other kids like you want to spend more time with you? That's right; you feel more confident because it feels great, doesn't it? Making new friends means they think you're fantastic, and that's how you feel about yourself, right?

It's Fun: You've probably already figured out that being creative is super fun. But did you know that having fun can make you more confident? Oh yes, it sure can! Isn't that excellent news? Having fun can make you more confident because you're doing something that makes you feel good inside and makes you happy. When you're joyful and happy, you start believing in yourself and your abilities. Remember, believing in yourself is the second confidence tool.

♥ ❤ ♥ ❤ ♥ ❤ ♥

Everybody is Creative – Do Not Let Anyone Tell You Otherwise

I want to make it clear to you that EVERYONE is creative! When you think of creative people, you might think of people who can dance, sing, act, or draw well. But that's just one part of creativity. As I said earlier, creativity is also about coming up with new ideas and solving problems, and

EVERYONE knows how to do this, including you, my dear friend.

Think about the last time you had to come up with a new idea or solve a problem. Maybe you had too many clothes in your wardrobe and had to figure out how to organize them. Or your teacher gave you some homework to do that was a bit hard, and you had to think about the best way to get it done. I know there's something you've had to do that involves being creative. Please do me a favor; get yourself a pen and paper. Write down the things you've had to do that involved using your creativity. I bet you'll write down a lot of stuff.

If you don't think you're a creative person, I bet you've got a lot of interests and passions, right? Maybe you love cooking or sewing with your mom, planting fruits and vegetables in the garden, cheerleading, or you like playing a specific sport. Whatever it is that you like doing, guess what? You need to be creative to do it. For example, coming up with new recipes to cook with your mom, thinking about the best way to plant your fruits and vegetables, or thinking about new skills to use when you're cheerleading or playing the sports you're into. These things make you very creative.

Another cool thing about creativity is that it's like a muscle; the more you use it, the more it grows. Even if you don't think you're very creative at the moment, keep practicing, and it won't be long before you're a creative genius.

What I want you to remember is that creativity is about using your imagination to come up with new ideas, solve problems, and express yourself in your own way.

THE SECRET TOOL: CREATIVITY   45

The girl that runs faster than boys.

Sportswear Style

There is no right or wrong way to be creative, so don't be afraid to show your creativity and see what amazing things you can do.

How Clothes Can Affect Your Confidence

Let me tell you a short story about myself. When I was around nine or ten years old, sometimes I was not too fond of the clothes my mom wanted me to wear. When I was wearing something I didn't like, I walked with my head down because I didn't feel good about myself. But when I wore something I liked, I walked with my head high towards the sky because I felt happy, and when I looked in the mirror, I was pleased with what I saw. I didn't know it then, but my clothes helped me to have confidence, and your clothes will help you to have confidence, too; let me tell you why.

You Get to Express Yourself: Did you know that the clothes you wear help you show a part of your personality? Let's say you're into sports; when you look like a skateboarding pro, people will know you love to skate. Wearing clothes that help you express yourself is a great way to make friends because people don't have to guess what you're into. It's almost like a secret code, and you all recognize each other when you see each other.

You Feel Important and Special: I'm sure you've gotten all dressed up for a special occasion before, such as a birthday, a wedding, or Christmas. It felt good, didn't it? I remember how I felt when I was a little girl, and I got dressed up for special occasions. When I pulled the outfit I loved out of the wardrobe, put it on, and looked at myself in the mirror. I thought to myself with a big smile on my face, "I look wonderful!" I felt so good that sometimes I wanted to wear the outfit to bed, but my mom wouldn't let me.

Tell me something, how did you feel the last time you wore your favorite outfit? You felt really good and happy, didn't you? You gain more confidence when you feel great and unique because you feel proud of who you are, smile more, are more friendly, and feel great. When you feel this way about yourself, it makes you more confident.

You Feel Comfortable: One day, I saw a video about a little boy of about five years old getting dressed to go to a wedding. He was wearing a suit, a shirt, a tie, trousers, and a waist jacket. He was crying as his mom was putting his clothes on; he kept saying he didn't want to wear the suit because he didn't like how it looked on him. The little boy was crying because he didn't feel comfortable in the suit. I was amazed because, at such a young age, he knew what he wanted, and that was to feel comfortable in what he was wearing. When you feel comfortable, you feel confident because the clothes make you feel good, and when you look in the mirror, you like what you see.

You Make Friends: Everyone has their own unique style of dressing. When you wear clothes that you like and you feel confident, people will say, "Hey, look at her; she looks amazing!" Then they'll come up to you and ask where you got your outfit from and what made you choose it. People will notice you because of how you dress, and you'll make friends with kids who have the same taste in clothes as you do.

Although clothes can make you feel more confident, they are just clothes, and you shouldn't allow them to change who you are. You're still amazing, no matter what you're wearing. But when you want to feel more confident, wear clothes that make you feel good about yourself.

How did you enjoy chapter four? There was a lot to learn, right? So that you don't forget, here's a quick reminder of everything you've just read:

- Creativity is the third confidence tool.
- Creativity is about using your imagination to create something unique and new.
- Being creative is also about being able to solve problems and come up with amazing or unique ideas.
- Being creative lets you express yourself the way you want to.
- Creativity can boost your confidence because you've got to challenge yourself.
- Everyone is creative, not just people with special talents.
- Clothes can affect your confidence because you get to express yourself.

Do you get bored with the clothes you wear sometimes? If you want to find your style, have a read through the next chapter, and decide what styles you like the best. Then have a chat with your parents about it. If they are okay with it, they will help you create the look you want.

Chapter 5

5

From Boring to Stylish

"Style is something each of us already has, all we need to do is find it." ~ DVF

H I, IT'S LEONORA AGAIN; I hope you're enjoying the book because I love it. I can't wait to get started with helping you find your unique style. But before we do this, I want to say this. If you want to be confident, it's really important that you are unique and that you don't follow every trend that comes out. Being confident is about having your own style and expressing your personality. When you follow every trend, you're trying to keep up with a common look.

When you see something you like, you take ideas from that look and make it your own. Make sense?

Okay, cool, now I want you to answer these questions for me so you can help me understand a bit more about your style:

- How would you describe your personal style?
- What type of clothes do you feel most comfortable in?
- Are there any famous people or influencers whose style you admire?
- Are there any colors or patterns you don't like wearing?
- Do you enjoy wearing any jewelry pieces or accessories to complete your outfits?
- What is your favorite type of shoes to wear (boots, sneakers, sandals)?
- What's your favorite clothing type (sweatshirts, t-shirts, dresses)?
- Do you like wearing more comfortable, fitted, or loose clothes?
- What's your favorite color to wear?
- What's your favorite pattern to wear?

That's all my questions for you now, but I'll probably ask you some more later. I hope you have fun answering them. I'll speak to you soon...

The Clothes You Choose Say a Lot About the Person You Are

You'll meet Leonora again shortly because she will help you become a very stylish girl! Okay, great, let us talk a bit about why your clothes say a lot about the person you are.

Expressing Your Personality: What you wear is a way of expressing your personality. For example, if you're shy and don't like being the center of attention, you'll wear simple clothes that make you blend in with everyone else. But if you're loud and outgoing, you might wear bright clothes that make you stand out.

Your Interests: The clothes you wear say a lot about the things you're interested in. For example, if you wear an anime graphic t-shirt, people will know you are an anime fan. If you wear a sweatshirt with your favorite sports team on the front, people will know you're a fan of that sports team. People might think you're artistic and creative if you like wearing clothes with patterns or cool designs.

Your Mood: Even if you don't do it on purpose, the colors you wear say a lot about your mood, and some people will think you're in a certain mood because of the colors you're wearing. For example, if you're wearing bright pink, orange, or yellow, people might think you're happy and outgoing. But if you wear dark colors like black, brown, and navy blue, people might assume you're a bit more serious.

Different Style Examples

There are a lot of different clothing styles that you might need to learn about. Also, you could be wearing some of these items now and not know they are popular in a specific style. In this book, you will see the nine fashion styles that Leonora will be wearing to help you decide what kind of clothing styles you like best. Experiment with different styles. Choose the clothes that make you feel happy and comfortable and will reflect who you are. If you do this, you will find your unique style that will boost your confidence. Pay attention!

Streetwear: Includes comfortable, casual clothes with bright colors and strong artwork. Here are some clothes you might wear if you are going for the streetwear look:

- **Hoodies:** You'll see people in streetwear fashion wearing oversized or cropped (cut short, reveals the stomach a little) hoodies with pictures or writing on the front.

- **Sneakers:** Sneakers are trendy.

- **T-Shirts:** T-shirts with writing or pictures are another excellent item.

- **Baseball Caps:** You'll often see people in streetwear fashion wear baseball caps.

- **Varsity Jackets:** Very popular.

Sportswear: The sportswear style is all about looking athletic and feeling comfortable at the same time. You'll see people wearing clothes like:

- **Sneakers:** They're comfortable to wear and support your feet so you can run and play sports.

- **Sweatpants/Sweatshirts:** Sweatpants and sweatshirts look really cool, but they're also really cozy and comfortable. They're great for keeping warm after playing sports or at home.

- **Tank tops/T-shirts:** These clothing items are also really comfortable, and they have cool designs on them.

- **Athletic shorts:** Athletic shorts come in many cool colors and designs. They can be just above your knees or past your knees.

Girly Style: The girly dress is cute, fashionable, and feminine. Some popular features of the girly style include:

- **Colorful, Fun, Prints:** Clothes with a girly style usually have bright colors with fun prints like stripes, polka dots, and flowers.

- **Lace and Ruffles:** Lace and ruffles look really pretty and feel good to the touch when you're wearing them.

- **Flouncy Skirts/Dresses:** Skirts and dresses that are full and flouncy are also popular for girly styles.

- **Cute Details:** Girly clothes have a lot of cute details on them, like sequins, ribbons, or bows.

Skateboarders: Skateboarders wear clothes that allow them to move quickly and comfortably. Here are some examples of how skateboarders like to dress:

- **Protective Gear:** Protective gear such as elbow pads, knee pads, and helmets keep skateboarders safe so they don't hurt themselves while skating.

- **Beanies and Hats:** Hats and beanies are popular. Obviously, they're stylish, but also because they help them stay warm in colder weather and keep the sun out of their eyes.

- **Sneakers:** Skateboarders like wearing trendy sneakers made by popular brands. Also, they must choose sneakers with a good grip and a flat sole to be safe on their skateboard.

- **Jeans and Shorts:** Skateboarders usually wear loose-fitting jeans and shorts to move around quickly on their skateboards. But if they're not skateboarding, many skateboarders like wearing skinny jeans.

- **T-Shirts:** Skateboarders wear loose-fitting t-shirts that might have a picture or writing on the front displaying their favorite brands or words about skating.

Hip-hop Style: Hip-hop is a type of music, and the people who make hip-hop music usually dress in a certain way. It's trendy and cool; hip-hop-style clothing creates a unique look that shows your love for the music. Here are a few examples of the hip-hop style:

- **Baseball Caps:** Baseball caps are popular in the hip-hop style; some people like to wear them backward.

- **Hoodies:** Hip-hop style hoodies are usually baggy (oversized, comfy).

- **Sneakers:** Sneakers give the outfit a cool look and are comfortable.

- **Baggy Clothes:** Hip-hop artists do a lot of dancing, so wearing baggy (oversized) clothes helps them move around.

Nerdy: You might have heard some people in your school being called 'nerds' because they get excellent grades and look a certain way. You might say that Harry Potter looks like a nerd. Being a nerd is cool; it means you're clever and know what you want, which is why the nerdy look has become so popular. Here are some examples of the clothes you would wear to create the nerdy look:

- **Bowties:** Bowties are a popular nerdy accessory; you can wear them with a button-up shirt, a sweater vest, or even a t-shirt.

- **Glasses:** People who dress in a nerdy style wear glasses even if they don't have bad eyesight.

- **Button-Up Shirts:** Button-up shirts with prints or patterns are a popular choice for those who like the nerdy style.

- **T-Shirts:** A nerdy style t-shirt might have words or pictures on it related to being clever.

The girl that embraces her strengths and accepts her weaknesses

Hip-Hop Style

Bohemian: The bohemian style is also called "boho," it's about expressing that you are a free spirit and live a carefree lifestyle.

- **Loose-Fitting Tops:** Bohemian style tops are flowy and loose-fitting

- **Embroidery:** Embroidery is decorating material like sequins, buttons and making patterns with a needle and thread. Embroidery gives whatever you're wearing a unique look and makes it stand out.

- **Flowy Dresses/Skirts:** The dresses and skirts are usually flowy with bright or strong patterns.

Kawaii: You might wear Kawaii-style dresses, but you don't know what it actually means, so I'll tell you. 'Kawaii' is a Japanese word. It means 'cute' or 'adorable.' Isn't that cute? Do you want to be cute and adorable? If so, kawaii is your style. Here are some examples of the clothes you would wear to create the Kawaii style:

- Jumpsuits with a playful design.

- Oversized t-shirt dresses with cute words or pictures with pleated skirts.

- Skater dresses with playful patterns like cartoon characters, stripes, and polka dots.

- Baby doll dresses with bows, lace, ruffles, and pastel colors.

Rock Style: Here are some examples of the clothes you would wear to create the rock-style look:

- A black fake leather jacket
- A blue denim jacket.
- A t-shirt with a picture of your favorite band.
- Your favorite jeans.
- Ankle boots

The cool thing about knowing about all these different styles is that you don't have to stick to just one. One day you might feel like looking nerdy; the next, like a skateboarder, and on another day, you might want to dress in a girly style. Basically, dress how you feel and not how you think other people expect you to dress.

Here's a quick reminder of what you've just read and the 9 styles you'll see Leonora wearing and that you might like to wear yourself:

- The clothes you choose say a lot about the person you are because you get to express your personality, your interests, and your mood.
- These are some styles to wear, including streetwear, sportswear, girly, hip-hop, nerdy, bohemian, kawaii, skateboarder, and rock style. There are more fashion

styles, but I chose the most appropriate for tween girls.

Fashion can make you experiment and be creative. Trying different styles can be fun. Step out of your comfort zone with new looks and get more confidence.

In chapter six, you'll learn how to start putting your unique style together by doing something exciting. I know you're going to love it!

Chapter 6

6

How to Make a Fashion Mood Board & Develop Your Style

"Confidence. If you have it, you can make anything look good." ~ DVF

SO NOW THAT YOU know about all the styles, it's time to create your own fashion mood board. In case you don't know what a fashion mood board is, let me tell you all about it.

Okay, you remember me telling you I used to be a fashion designer, right? Well, when we're designing clothes, the first stage is to make a mood board (collage), and we show the mood board to the stores or clients. Sometimes they love it, others not so much. If they like our inspiration on the mood board, they will buy our collection of clothes. If they do not like it very much, we will make some changes together.

The mood board is like a big collage (a collage is a collection of pictures and images glued onto a sheet of paper). On the board, you put pictures of clothes you might have printed off the internet or cut out of newspapers, magazines, and drawings. It can also have different colors, fabrics, textures, and photos or pictures of hairstyles that you like. Basically, anything that will help you express yourself.

Everything you add to your fashion mood board will give you a better idea of what you want your style to be. You know, because it's great to have an idea in your head and see it in real life, right? And that's what a fashion mood board helps you to do. Clarify your vision or style that you want to express.

But the best part is that you will show the mood board to your mom. She can be the store or the client and tell you whether she likes it or not. If she likes your mood board, great. If not, then create a mood board together with a more appropriate style for your age. When it is time to buy and choose your clothes, your mom and you will have a better understanding of what you like.

Fashion Mood Board Pieces (COLLAGE)

What you put on your mood board is up to you, but here is a list of the materials:

Photos: You can take the pictures yourself or have your mom or another adult take them for you. For example, when you go to a store, and you see something that inspires you. Or a friend or a family member might be wearing something that you like.

Drawings: If you can't find an exact picture of what you have in your mind on the internet or in a magazine, you can draw it.

Colors: You can use your favorite colors and paint them on the board with markers or crayons.

Text: The text will help describe your thinking. For example, you might have words like happy, colorful, pretty cool, stellar, dynamite, incredible, sensational, fantastic, informal, and wonderful.

Texture: Mood boards look great when they're decorated with things from nature or everyday life, such as flowers, plants, burnt paper, fabric, pieces of wood, airplane tickets, and pieces of magazines.

How to Make a Fashion Mood Board

Now that you know what a fashion mood board is and the pieces you'll need, it's time to make one. Are you ready?

Step 1: Get Ideas – What words and ideas come to mind when you think about a fashion mood board? They could be words such as stylish, cool, trends, colors, and clothes.

Step 2: Decide on the Board – Decide on the board you'll use for your fashion mood board. You can make it on a hard board or a foam board. If you're unsure, you might want to go to the store to get a better idea of what the boards are like.

Step 3: Get Inspiration - You can get inspiration from anywhere, from TV, music, your friends, actresses, models, sports players, cartoons, anime, and nature.

Step 4: Gather Your Materials - Once you've decided on what you're going to do with your mood board, it's time to start gathering the materials. This is what you'll need (you might not use all of the items, but I'm giving you an idea).

- The board
- Glue
- Scissors
- Magazines
- Newspapers
- Pictures
- Fabrics
- Things you've collected from outside
- Markers/pens/pencils
- Colored pencils
- Ruler
- Buttons
- Sequins/glitter/ribbons
- Examples of different colors

Step 5: Test What Works – Your fashion mood board will take some effort to make, and it's okay if you start it and decide you don't like the way it looks and want to start again. You can start again as many times as you need to until you're happy with the way it looks. The mood board will express your unique style.

How to Create Your Own Style

Hey girlies, it's me, Leonora; again, I hope you had fun reading about all the different styles and the fashion mood board. I've got a mood board, and I love it. Well, the first mood board that I made, my mother did not like it very much. She told me that I had too much black in my mood board. I love the color black; I know it's a little strange for somebody who is 11 years old.

Together we added more colors that were better for my age. But we left some black on the mood board, and that made me very happy. In the end, my mother and I were happy with the mood board. Sometimes I have different ideas, and I add or change the mood board, so you can do the same with yours.

Now, it's time for the really fun part, and that's learning how to create your own style. That's why I asked you all those questions earlier; it will make things a lot easier for you.

But before we get started, I just want you to know that even though I've always loved fashion, I didn't really know how to dress, and it took me a while to create my own style.

I want to make your style easy for you, and that's why I'm here to help. So, are you ready to create your own style? Okay, let's get started.

Actually, let me say this before we get started. I'm only 11 years old, and because I'm so young, I had to get my mom involved in creating my style. My mom wanted me to be happy, so she was okay with most stuff, but she wasn't okay with some of my clothes because she said I was too young for them.

So before you get started, please ask your mom, I'm sure she'll be happy with whatever you choose, but you just want to make sure, okay?

Start With What You Like

Until I was eight, my mom chose all my clothes; sometimes, I didn't like them. I mean, I was grateful that my mom bought me clothes, but when I looked in the mirror, sometimes I did not feel confident. I did not want to tell her that I was not too fond of the clothes she bought me because I didn't want to hurt her feelings. Instead, I told her that I wanted to start buying (of course, with her help) my own clothes.

Of course, she wanted to know where I was going to get the money from. So that's when I told her I wanted to start washing our cars and helping more around the house. She wasn't too happy with the idea at first, but I talked her into it, and yeah, that's how I started making a small amount of money.

Later my mother was very happy with her decision because she saw that I was learning to save money and making decisions about my clothes with her help. If your story is similar to mine, you might want to do what I did.

Anyway, go into your wardrobe, pull out all your favorite clothes and shoes, and arrange your clothes on your bed and your shoes on the floor. Then get a notepad and pen and write a list of all your favorite clothes and shoes and why you like wearing them. Write about how they make you feel when you wear them.

Then please put those clothes and shoes back and remove all the clothes and shoes you don't like wearing. Like before, arrange the clothes on your bed and the shoes on the floor.

Write a list of all the clothes and shoes you don't like, why you don't like wearing them, and how they make you feel when you do wear them. Put everything back in the wardrobe because soon I'm going to tell you how you can turn some of the clothes you don't like into unique items.

So now you know exactly what you like and what you don't like in your wardrobe.

Creating a fashion style takes time. Try out different combinations of clothing pieces and see what you like. Wear outfits that make you happy and boost your confidence. No matter what you wear, wear it with confidence. Have fun with it.

Experiment With Different Styles

You should experiment with different styles because sometimes you just don't know what you're really into until you try it. I had no idea rock was my style until I tried it on; I was like, yep! This is me. I still mix and match, but my main style is rock. Remember the nine illustrated fashion styles that I am wearing. It could help you to understand your style a little better, or you can create your own unique style.

So this is what you do when you're getting inspiration from other people about how to dress. Look at the patterns, colors, and accessories and ask yourself do they look interesting, cool, or unique? What was the first thing that you noticed about their style?

Next, think about how you can add some of these things into your style. You could wear cute socks or add a pop of color with a scarf like the person you saw.

You can also get inspiration from fashion magazines and websites. They'll show you complete outfits and how to style and accessorize them.

Remember that inspiration doesn't mean copying other people; it means taking ideas from them and turning them into your own. Creating and understanding your own style will boost your confidence because confidence is about being unique and expressing yourself through your clothes.

♥ ♥ ♥ ♥ ♥

Use Your Secret Creativity Tool

Now this is where creating your style gets really exciting because you get to use your Secret Creativity Tool and express yourself the way you want. This is where you can really let your personality shine, and you'll be like a bright and shining star everywhere you go. Sounds cool, right?

Okay, so do you remember I told you not to throw your old clothes away because we're going to make them unique. Well, this is where it starts.

Add Funky Accessories: I absolutely love accessories because you can get dressed and think you don't like what you're wearing, but as soon as you add some accessories, the outfit goes from blah to WOW! Here are a few accessories I think you'd like:

- **Bright Belts:** Adding a bright belt will make you feel like you're wearing a whole new outfit.

- **Funky Sunglasses:** I love wearing oversized or colorful sunglasses; I feel so confident in them, and I'm pretty sure you will too.

- **Statement Hats:** You can wear funky hats.

- **Colorful Shoelaces:** Oh my goodness! Don't get rid of another pair of shoes until you've got some colorful shoelaces.

- **Add Pins:** Add cute pins onto your backpack or jacket to show off your personality.

- **Jewelry:** Wear funky earrings, necklaces, bracelets, or colorful accessories.

DIY Your Clothes: If you need to learn what DIY means, it means 'do it yourself.' This is where you can get super-duper creative and totally transform some of the clothes you don't like. Okay, here are a few tips:

- **Add Embroidery:** If you want to give your clothes a one-of-a-kind look, add some embroidery to them using sequins or buttons. Ask your mother for some help.

- **Add Patches:** Patches are the coolest thing ever! You can sew or iron them onto your clothes. But make sure you ask your mom before you do this and that she's there with you because irons are hot.

- **Fabric Markers:** It's the coolest thing ever to use fabric markers on your clothes. They come in various colors and styles; some are permanent, and others come out in the wash. Before drawing on your clothes, plan the design on paper. It might take two, three, or even four tries before you get it right, but you want to make sure it's perfect before you draw the design onto your clothes, or you might get it wrong. Get all the colors you need and start practicing. Once you've created your unique design, carefully draw it onto your clothes.

HOW TO MAKE A FASHION MOOD BOARD & DEVELOP YOUR STYLE 73

The girl who owns a colorful gallery of her own artwork

Boho style

- **Non-Toxic Washable Paint:** Non-toxic means that the paint isn't dangerous, won't make you sick, and is safe to use. But it would help to be more careful when using paint because it can get messy. The process is the same as with the fabric markers; you create your unique design on paper first. Once you're happy with it, paint it onto your clothes. There are loads of colors to choose from. But before you get started, place a sheet of cardboard under the clothes so the paint doesn't go through the material. Once you're done, leave the clothes in the same spot to dry.

- **Decorate:** You can also decorate your clothes with rhinestones, studs, sequins, ribbons, buttons, and beads. You'll need to go with your mom to the store to get powerful glue so your decorations stick to the clothes properly.

- **Try Different Hairstyles:** I love putting my hair in different styles.

How to Style Your Clothes

Styling your clothes is so much fun. You can do a lot more with your outfits than you think. Here are some tips:

- Add a pop of color to a light-colored outfit with colorful sneakers or jewelry.

- Mix patterns by pairing floral shorts with a striped top.

- Style a jumpsuit with a denim jacket and sneakers

- Pull the waist of a dress in by adding a belt to it.
- Pair solid-colored leggings with a printed top.
- Knot a button-up shirt over a graphic t-shirt and shorts.
- Layer a denim jacket over a floral dress.
- Do a French tuck with a graphic t-shirt into a skater skirt.

"What's a French tuck?" I hear you asking. Basically, a French tuck is when you tuck an oversized or looser top into a higher-rise bottom and let the back part of the top hang down.

Have Fun and Be Confident

Creating your own style is a really fun and exciting experience. Trust me, you're going to absolutely love it when everything starts coming together, and you start seeing how stylish you can really be. Finding your style is about being confident and doing what you love. It's not about trying to be the same as everyone else but about being unique and loving who you are so the world can see how awesome you are.

It's the most fantastic thing ever: expressing yourself the way you want to through your clothes. No more wearing the weird frilly dresses your mom buys you, ha ha ha. Unless you want to, that is. But anyway, once you get into creating your own style, you'll have an absolute blast!

I'm glad you made it to the end with me, and I hope you have started creating your style, looking fabulous, and gaining more and more confidence. In case you've forgotten some of the things we talked about, here's a quick reminder:

- A fashion mood board helps you express yourself and decide what style of clothes you want to wear.

- You create your style by starting with what you like and experimenting with different styles.

- Your secret creativity tool will help you add a personal touch to your clothes.

- There are a lot of different ways to style your clothes.

- Have fun and be confident when creating your own unique style.

DIY Birthday

Before I go, I want to give you an idea and tell you how I celebrate my birthday. This is what I do with Mom. My present is to go to a fabric store and buy the following: acrylic crystal beads, and rhinestones, get the cheap ones they work too, fabric with cool and artistic designs, ribbons, trims, buttons, and patches.

Then I called some friends, invited them to my birthday party, and told them to bring one piece of old clothing. Can you imagine the first time that I asked them to my party? They thought that I was teasing them. My friends came with their old clothes. We adorned and beautified the clothes with what I bought at the fabric store. It was awesome. We DIY our old clothes. Oh, remember the glue.

Before you read the next chapter, I want to tell you one more thing. Even though I do all this fashion stuff now, I never used to be very confident.

But do you want to know how I became confident? I practiced! And in chapter seven, I'll tell you all about it, see you there!

Chapter 7

7

Practice Confidence

"Happiness and confidence are the prettiest things you can wear." ~ Taylor Swift

Hi, it's me, Leonora, again. I want to start by introducing you to my dog Rocco. He's so cute, and I love him with all my heart. When I'm not in school, he follows me everywhere. I take him for a walk every morning and every evening with my mom. He's here with me now as I'm writing this; you can see him in one of the illustrations.

Rocco helped me to become more confident because I take care of him. I feed him, give him water to drink, bathe him, and, as I said, I take him for walks. Taking care of Rocco lets me know that my mom thinks I'm responsible, and that makes me really happy.

So, do you remember that I said that I haven't always been confident? Well, I'm confident now because I spent a lot of time practicing, and I still practice being confident. In this chapter, I want to show you how and I'm going to let Marta tell you all about it.

Daily Exercises to Practice Your Confidence

Do you remember that I said that confidence is like a muscle? That's because the more you use it, the bigger it grows, and that's why you've got to practice being confident so that you can get more and more confident every day. Don't worry if you don't feel confident right now; that's fine; keep practicing. You'll soon be able to say confidently that you're confident. Give me a virtual high-five if you're ready to practice being confident!

Be Positive: Being positive means that you try and find something to be happy about instead of thinking about all the stuff you're not happy about. Leonora told me that one day, she had a stomachache and didn't feel well. She had to take the day off school so she could get better. Leonora wasn't very happy about this because it was Pajama Day at school, and she was going to miss it. This is a student fundraising idea to collect donations for children in exchange for them coming to school in pajamas for one day.

Of course, Leonora was upset because she was going to miss that fun day. But instead of thinking about her stomachache and missing the pajama day, Leonora thought about how grateful she was to have a mother who loved her and looked after her when she was sick. When she thought about all the good things she had in her life, it made her feel good about herself, and when you feel good about yourself, you're a lot more confident. So the next time something happens that you're not happy about, think about the good things in your life, such as your brothers and sisters, all the possible fun days, and the nice friends you have.

Look Good: How do you feel when you wear the clothes you like? Good right? Yes, that's because when you look good, you feel good. When you look in the mirror and like what you see, you smile and feel happy that you're wearing a nice outfit. I know you can't always wear your favorite clothes because you might have to wear a uniform to go to school. But make an effort, do your hair nicely, and wear some cool hair bands. If you don't wear a uniform to school, jazz things up a bit and wear something comfortable that you like, and that will make you happy at school. Then on the weekends, you can get creative and wear a fabulous outfit that will make you feel satisfied and confident.

Eat Well: Hi, it's Leonora. I love eating sweets, cakes, chocolates, and other yummy stuff. And I wouldn't say I liked it when my mom told me to eat vegetables because I think cake tastes much better. But one day, the tooth at the back of my mouth started hurting, and I had to go to the dentist and have it pulled out because all the sugar from the cakes and the sweets I was eating had made my teeth rot.

I wasn't very happy about that at all because I like my teeth, and I'd rather they were all in my mouth. After that, I decided to start eating my vegetables and more healthy stuff like my mom told me to. Guess what? It made me feel really amazing. And you know what happens when you feel amazing right? You have more confidence! When I started eating healthy stuff, I noticed that I wasn't so tired all the time, and I found it a lot easier to get things done. So now I don't want to sit in front of the TV until bedtime eating snacks; I want to be creative and make clothes or help my mother around the studio. Here are a few ideas to help you eat better:

- **Vegetables:** Eat more vegetables with your dinner.
- **Fruits:** After dinner, have a piece of fruit instead of a slice of cake.
- **Water:** Instead of drinking sugary drinks all the time, drink more water.
- **Snacks:** Instead of eating chips and chocolate for snacks, eat stuff like nuts, yogurt, and rice cakes.
- **Fast Food:** I used to eat fast food twice a week. Now I only eat one fast food meal every two weeks.

The healthier you eat, the better you'll feel; the better you feel, the more confident you'll be. And that's what we're aiming for, isn't it? I hope I've helped.

♥ ♥ ♥ ♥ ♥

Keep a Daily Journal: Keeping a daily journal is so much fun, and I can tell you that you will love it. Rocco says, "Hi" By the way, he's sooo cute! Let me tell you why writing a journal is so awesome. Your journal sort of becomes your best friend. Not only does it help you become a better writer, but you can tell your journal anything and talk about things you don't feel comfortable discussing with anyone else. Okay, so are you ready to get started writing your journal? Good, here's how to do it:

- **Choose a Journal:** Choosing a journal is fun because there are so many to choose from. You can even buy a plain one and decorate it.

- **Choose a Time:** I prefer to write in my journal after dinner. You can choose whatever time you like.

- **Write:** You can write about anything in your journal. I write about things like how my day at school went and how I'm feeling about different things.

- **Draw**: I love drawing, so I draw a lot of pictures in my journal. If you like drawing, you can draw some too.

- **Set Goals:** It's really important to set goals so all your dreams can come true. Write all your goals down in your journal.

- **Keep it Private:** Your journal is your private book to write about things that are important to you. I don't show what I've written in my journal to my friends; it's my special book.

Keeping a journal makes me more confident because it gives me a safe space to express how I feel. It makes me feel strong and brave because it takes a strong person to talk about how they really feel. Here's Marta again.

Speak Kindly to Yourself: Speaking kindly to yourself every day will make you more confident because you are saying nice things about yourself. There are some days when you don't feel your best. Maybe you didn't get a good grade at school, or you had an argument with a friend. But when you say nice things to yourself, you feel better. Don't just speak kindly to yourself when you're not having a great day; speak kindly to yourself every day. Here are some nice words you can say to yourself:

- I can do it.
- I am special and unique.
- I am confident and brave.
- I am proud of everything I've achieved.

Mirror Exercise: We look in the mirror every day to check that we look okay; but did you know that you can use a mirror for more than just checking what you look like? Yes, you can. You can use your mirror to become more confident. That's amazing, right? Let me tell you how. When you look in the mirror, you can look at everything you're proud of. To do the mirror exercise, you'll need to stand in front of the mirror and speak to yourself out loud. Here are some of the things you can say:

- I am proud of how I styled my hair today.
- I am proud of the t-shirt I made.

- I am proud that I got a good grade on my math homework.

You can do this exercise by making a list of all the things you're proud of about yourself and then stand in front of a mirror and read the list out aloud. Once you've finished the exercise, ask yourself how you feel and think about why you feel this way. For example, you might feel happy, proud, or grateful.

Smile and Laugh: Do you love to smile and laugh? I know I do. But did you know that smiling and laughing can make you more confident? Yes, it can. You're more likely to smile and laugh when you're around friends and family. But what happens when you're alone? Here are a few ways to make yourself smile and laugh:

- Tell yourself a joke
- Remember something funny
- Watch something funny

Speak Up in Class: How do you feel about speaking up in class? I know that some kids don't like it because they don't want to say the wrong thing. But there's no such thing as saying the wrong thing because everyone has their own way of expressing their ideas. Speaking up in class makes you more confident because when you share your ideas in front of the class, you're showing that you have something important to say. Your teacher and other students in your class will listen and respond to what you say. The more you raise your hand in class, the more confident you'll become, especially when your friends and teachers tell you that they like what you said.

Practice Walking on a Runway: My mom and I have just taken Rocco for a walk. It was so much fun because we played catch. He has a little ball that he likes to play with. We go to the park, and I throw the ball far, and he runs fast and collects it, and brings it back to me.

Anyway, remember I said I was really nervous before I did the fashion show? Well, one of the things that made me more confident was practicing walking in my house.

I walked down the hall of my house and pretended I was on stage. It really helped. I put a mirror at the end of the hall so that I could see myself walking and so that I'd know what I needed to do to get better. Every time I walked, I had to remember to keep my back straight and my head up and have a positive attitude, even though I felt nervous.

But let me tell you the most important thing. When I have to walk in front of so many people, Marta told me to think of things I love doing, like walking Rocco or riding a bike. When I do that, I forget about the people watching me and I don't get nervous. If you are doing something that makes you a little nervous, think of things you love to do, and you will not be that nervous. Try it; it feels really good.

PRACTICE CONFIDENCE 87

The girl that loves what she does

Skateboard style

Be Friends With Nice People: When you have nice friends, they're supportive and kind and make you feel important and valued. Think about it like this, imagine you come into school with your backpack that you spent the night decorating with different materials. You're really proud, and you can't wait to show it to your friends. When you show the backpack to your friends, they say, "Wow, it looks AWESOME. This makes you feel proud of your work and happy, right? Exactly! That's why you need to have nice friends, because they support and encourage you and make you feel more confident in yourself and your abilities.

Hi, it's Leonora again. You've got a lot of stuff to practice with to help you become more confident. You must practice every day; you don't need to do everything, but pick one or two things to do every day and stick to it. I found it helpful to have a practice chart.

After you've chosen the two things from what you've just read, get a sheet of paper and write them at the top of the paper. Then write the numbers one to thirty underneath. Stick the paper on your wall, and every day, once you've finished your confidence exercises, cross off one day. Trust me, by the time you've crossed out thirty days, you'll be a lot more confident.

So that you don't forget, here's a quick reminder of everything you've learned in this chapter:

- The more you practice being confident, the more confident you'll become.

- Look good by wearing the clothes that make you feel the most confident.

- Eat more fruits, vegetables, and healthy snacks. Don't eat too much fast food.

- Keep a daily journal and write about all the things that are important to you.

- Speak kindly to yourself with words that make you feel happy and positive.

- Look in the mirror every day and tell yourself you're proud of yourself.

- Smile and laugh by telling yourself jokes.

In the next chapter, you're going to learn about something really great. It's the fourth confidence tool, and it's super important. If you want to know what it is, keep reading.

Chapter 8

8

Social Confidence

"I believe you learn social skills by mixing with people." ~ Joe Morgan

HEY, I HOPE YOU'RE doing great and ready to learn all about the fourth confidence tool, social skills. Did you know that social skills are like a superpower? They can help you connect and make friends, have great relationships, and feel more CONFIDENT about meeting new people. Have you ever been to a friend's birthday party and felt a bit nervous because there were a lot of new kids there that you didn't know? Well, you'll never have to worry about feeling like that again because, in this chapter, you're going to learn all about social skills and how to boost your social confidence.

What Are Social Skills?

Social skills are all about understanding how we express ourselves and act around other people. It's about treating everyone with respect and kindness. When you have good social skills, you can talk with other people and listen to them in a way that makes them feel good and heard. This skill, or superpower as I like to call it, is a superpower that makes you socially Confident. When you were little, your mom probably taught you how to introduce yourself when you met someone new. Maybe she told you to give a friendly smile, shake hands and say polite words like "please" and "thank you" to show your appreciation and gratitude. Your mom might have also taught you how to listen properly to what other people were saying, and when it's your turn to speak, say things in a way that shows you care.

Social skills are also about understanding how other people feel and showing that you understand by being kind and loving. It's about being patient with the kids who need help understanding things as quickly as we'd like, and making sure that everyone feels good and included. Sometimes, you might not agree with what someone says, and that's fine. Just think how boring the world would be if everyone had the exact same things to say all the time. I wouldn't like that, would you? When you have good social skills, you know how to get along with people even if you don't agree with them. Having good social skills means everyone is happy because you can discuss things and find solutions.

♥ ♥ ♥ ♥ ♥

SOCIAL CONFIDENCE 93

I love being Brainy

Nerd Style

Types of Social Skills

There are a lot of different social skills you can learn. When you get older, you'll know more about social skills, but the ones I'm going to talk about now will help you a lot.

Speaking: Just like being creative, speaking is a magical way of expressing yourself. It's like having a secret treasure chest full of words that you can open whenever you want to tell someone something. It's how you share your thoughts, feelings, and ideas with others. Whether you're happy, sad, curious, or excited, speaking is how you let it all out so that everyone can hear your voice.

Speaking is also like a special bridge that connects you to the people you want to talk to. It lets you share stories, ask questions, and learn from other people.

One of the coolest things about speaking is that you can share stories with people. Stories are fantastic because they can be about many different things, like dreams and adventures. By telling stories, we take others on a magical journey where we can make them smile and laugh.

Do you like learning about exciting stuff? I do, and so does Leonora. I'll let her tell you all about why she likes learning exciting stuff.

Hi friends! Leonora has entered the chat again. I've just finished feeding my dog, Rocco. He was really hungry and ate all the food, ha ha ha. I love watching Rocco eat; when his food is ready, he gets excited and wags his tail fast. But the interesting part is when I forget that it is his time to eat he stands before me and stares for a long time. He does not bark; he stares into my eyes like he wants to say something. Then I remember. Sorry, Rocco, I forgot it is time to have your "pollito" chicken food. Then after we run together I feed him his "pollito." Believe me, Rocco understands English and Spanish.

Okay, so in case you're wondering what Rocco has to do with learning, let me tell you. So do you remember that I said I got Rocco for my birthday? I begged and pleaded with my mom and dad to get him, and they said I could get one if I learned everything there was to know about taking care of a dog. I promised my parents I would start learning about dogs, and that's what I did. My mom found a lot of videos for me to watch on the internet, and I read some books about looking after dogs.

But the most exciting thing I learned about dogs was from an old lady named Hilda, who lives across the street from me. She has a big brown dog named Cleopatra, who I love very much. She and Rocco are best friends now, and sometimes we all go on walks together, and Cleopatra and Rocco play together in the park. Although the books and videos were good, and I learned a lot from them, and the people who wrote them are really clever, Hilda taught me a lot about dogs.

But the main reason I learned so much from her was because I could ask her questions. My mom and I went to Hilda's house every Friday night to learn about dogs, and I always had a list of questions with me.

As I said, the videos and the books were good, but I couldn't ask any questions, and that's how you learn interesting stuff, by asking questions. Asking Hilda questions also gave me more confidence about asking questions in class because any time I asked Hilda something, she would always say, "That's an excellent question, Leonora; I had never thought about that before."

After that, I started asking more questions in class, and my teacher was really pleased with me because it showed that I wanted to learn more. So girly, ask more questions when you're speaking to someone, and you'll learn a lot more, okay? That's all I've got to say for now, it was great talking to you again, and I'll be back soon! Here's Marta.

♥ ♥ ♥ ♥ ♥

Leonora is so amazing, isn't she? I hope you've learned a lot from her because I definitely have. The more you practice speaking, the better you'll become at it. Here are some tips on how to become a better speaker:

- **Read More:** The more you read, the more words you'll learn, and the more words you know, the more you'll have to say when you speak.

- **Speak More:** Some children don't like speaking in front of the class because they don't want to get stuff wrong. But speaking in front of people is a great way to become a better speaker.

- **Listen More:** The more you listen to people who are good at speaking, the better you'll become at speaking. So spend more time listening to your parents, teachers, and anyone else who speaks well, and before you know it, you'll be an excellent speaker.

Listening: Now, let's talk about the two little things you have on the sides of your head. Can you guess what they are? Yep! Your ears. Because you're so smart, I'm sure you already know that your ears are for listening. But there's a lot more to listening than hearing with your ears; here's why listening is important:

- **Understanding Others:** Guess how you get to know people? By listening to them when they speak. Listening isn't just about hearing the special words that come out of a person's mouth; it's about understanding those words. When a person speaks, they're expressing their thoughts, feelings, and ideas. They're opening the door to their world, and you can step right in and learn all about them if you listen carefully. By truly listening, we show others that we respect and value them for who they are.

- **Better Relationships:** How would you feel if no one listened to you? If your friends, brothers, sisters, mom, and dad blocked their ears any time you wanted to speak to them? You wouldn't be very happy, would you? Not only would it make you feel sad, but it would also be very hard for them to get to know you. Please do me a favor and think about your best friend for a minute. Why did you become best friends? Because when you spoke to each other, you listened to each other and learned about each other, didn't you? You could have become best friends with anyone else in your class, but you chose your best friend because you liked a lot of the same stuff and you liked each other's personality. The only reason you felt so connected with your best friend is because you listened.

- **Learning:** Do you remember what Leonora said in the speaking section about how asking questions helped her to learn new things? So does listening. When you ask questions and the person you're asking gives you the information, you learn by listening to what they say. Listening is like an adventure because we get to explore new ideas and learn from others. When you listen to the teacher and your friends in class, and when you talk to older people who are really clever, like Leonora's friend Hilda, you learn a lot from them. When we listen, we learn about fascinating facts and stories that make us feel good. Listening helps us become smarter and wiser; it's like feeding our brain with all the yummy foods we like.

- **Solving Problems:** Have you watched the movie Superman? In case you haven't, a man named Clark Kent turns into Superman any time there's a problem, and he wears a cape that helps him fly so that he can quickly go and solve the problem. Listening is your own personal Superman cape for problem-solving. When people have thoughts and ideas, listening helps people come to an agreement that works for everyone. When you listen to the person you're speaking with and the other person listens when you talk, you can work together to find a solution.

- **Giving Support:** Have you ever come home from school feeling a bit sad? You might have received a low score on a test, and when you got home, you just wanted someone to speak to. Whether it was your brother, sister, mom, or dad, you wanted to tell someone all about the day you'd had and get them to give you a hug while they said special comforting words to make you feel better. Do the same and support others.

- **Speaking Better:** Have you heard some adults talk and think, "Wow, I can't wait until I'm an adult and can speak like that." The good news is that you can start to communicate better. Do you want to know the secret ingredient to speaking better? LISTENING! Why? Because the more you listen to other people talking, the more you learn about the type of language you should use.

- **Respecting Differences:** We are all unique; everyone has a special personality; people are different colors and have different ideas, experiences, and beliefs. Everyone has something important to give to the world, and that includes you. Listening makes everyone feel included.

So my friends, now that you know why listening is important, here are some tips on how to practice being a better listener:

- **Pay Attention:** When someone is speaking, give them your full attention. Don't look around the room or look at your watch. When someone is speaking, the only thing you should be doing is looking directly at them and listening.

- **No Interrupting:** Do you get excited when someone is talking and jump in to tell them what you are thinking? That's called interrupting, and it's bad manners. When you interrupt people while they're speaking, you make them think that what they're saying is unimportant. Even if you're excited and ready to say something, wait until the other person has finished speaking before you talk.

- **Ask Questions:** Asking questions is a great way to be a better listener. You've got to pay attention to what the person is saying so that you know what questions to ask.

- **Be Understanding:** When someone is speaking, and they're expressing feelings like happiness, excitement, or sadness, you need to listen to really understand how the person feels. The more you can understand how a person feels, the more your listening skills will improve.

So, my friends, these tips will help you to become an excellent listener. Remember, being a good listener is just as important as being a good speaker. So put on your listening ears and become the best listener you can be.

Being Funny: Anytime I would get sick when I was a little girl, my mom would do everything she could to make me laugh because she said laughter is the best medicine. I want you to get ready for a giggle-filled adventure as you learn about why being funny is a super important social skill to have.

- **Spreading Happiness:** Everyone in the whole wide world wants to be happy, and that's why being funny is like having a magic wand that sprinkles happiness everywhere you go. How do you feel when people make you laugh? You feel fantastic, right? That's why it's good to make people laugh; it fills the air with positive vibes. Have you ever noticed that when one person laughs, everyone starts laughing? Because that's what laughter does, it jumps from one person to the next.

- **Making Friends:** When you meet new people, and you laugh together, you're more likely to become friends because laughing feels good. Laughing also makes you feel comfortable with the people you're around. And guess what? You want to be around people who make you feel good and comfortable, right? Exactly! That's why being funny helps you to make more friends.

- **Making Life Easier:** Remember I said that laughing is the best medicine; it works for all situations. Anytime someone isn't feeling great, making them laugh will make them feel better immediately. It might not make the problem disappear, but at least the person can laugh even if they still feel a bit sad.

- **Being Creative:** Remember the third confidence tool was creativity? Well, there are many ways you can be creative, and one of them is being funny. When you're funny, you become more creative because you've got to think of more jokes and stories to make everyone laugh.

Everyone has a funny side to them, and that includes you. There are a lot of different ways you can be funnier, and I'm going to let Leonora tell you about the first one:

Hi guys, it's Leonora. I've just finished doing my math homework. It was a little bit hard, but I'm getting a lot better at it now. I've been doing a lot of practicing, and my grades have improved, so my parents are really happy with me.

So if you find any subject difficult, don't worry about it, just spend more time practicing and trust me, you'll get better quickly. Anyway, let me tell you all about how telling jokes can make you more of a funny person.

- **Share Jokes:** While we're on the subject of laughing, I thought I'd make you laugh, so here's a joke for you. How come Teddy Bears never want to eat anything?

Because they are always stuffed. Ha ha ha. Funny right? Guess where I got that joke? From my joke book. I've got a large joke book, and it's got 100 jokes in it. I read it all the time, and I've learned many jokes.

- One day, I visited a restaurant with my mom, her friend Jessica, and her son Simon. Simon was only four years old and wasn't very happy, so he was crying loudly in the restaurant. I asked Simon if he wanted to hear a joke, and through his loud crying, he said yes. So I told him one of the jokes I had learned in my jokes book, and his crying turned into laughter. Simon wanted to hear more and more jokes, and so I kept telling them, and he kept laughing. Simon wasn't the only person laughing; everyone was laughing because my mom and Jessica both found the jokes funny. Learn one joke a week, and all your friends will think you're really funny. I'll hand you over to Marta again. See you later!

- **Be Silly:** Leonora told you about telling jokes; now I'm going to tell you about being silly. Being silly and playful is a great way to be funnier. You can be silly by making silly voices, acting out funny situations with your friends, and playing silly games. Use your imagination and let your silliness shine through.

Manners: I'm sure everyone reading has good manners because your parents taught you all about it. But I want to teach you more about what it means to have good manners.

If you already know this stuff, it can be a reminder for you, but this is what it means to have good manners:

- **Respect People:** Having manners means treating everyone with respect. You must treat adults with respect, and when you're talking to them, you should call them 'sir' and 'ma'am.' You also show respect by using kind words when speaking to people. You should be nice to people all the time, even if you don't agree with them. Because remember, there's nothing wrong with people having different thoughts and ideas because everyone is different.

- **Table Manners:** Eating at the table is a special time to enjoy your food and have a nice time with friends and family. Having good table manners means you do things like wait for everyone else to be served before digging in. You chew with your mouth closed, use your knife and fork properly, say "please" when you want someone to pass you something, and say "thank you" to the person who prepared the meal. It will help if you had good table manners whenever you eat, including at home, school, at your friend's house, and when you go out to eat.

- **Respect Personal Space:** Everyone has their own personal space. If you have your own room, that's your personal space. Your parent's room is their personal space, and your brother and sister's room is their personal space. Good manners also involve respecting people's personal space. You can respect a person's personal space by knocking on the door and waiting patiently before going in. If you want to borrow something, ask before you take it, and leave things the way you found them. When you respect people's personal space, it shows that you value and care about the person.

- **Being Grateful:** Being grateful is like a magic potion that can make the world a lot brighter. When someone gives you something, no matter how small it is, it's good manners to say thank you. Expressing gratitude lets people know that you appreciate them.

- **Being Polite:** Good manners are also about how you talk to people. When you're speaking to someone, always use a friendly tone; and if someone is speaking to you, listen carefully to what they are saying. Don't interrupt people when they're talking; instead, wait your turn to share what you want to say. Being polite also means that you don't make fun of people or share gossip (spill the tea) about other people because it's not nice, and you wouldn't like it if it happened to you.

♥ ♥ ♥ ♥ ♥

Now that you know what it means to have good manners, here are some tips on how you can practice having good manners:

- **Teach Others:** Teach your friends about what it means to have good manners and make a deal with each other that you're always going to practice having good manners.

- **Be Polite:** Always say please and thank you, even if it seems like you don't need to say it.

- **Be Kind:** Being kind will always help you to have better manners because being kind means respecting people, and respecting people is really important when it comes to having good manners.

Now that you know all about social skills, guess what you're going to do? You're going to practice, practice, practice! Remember, the more you practice, the better your social skills will become, and it will help you gain more CONFIDENCE. So that you don't forget what you've just read, here's a quick reminder:

- Social skills are all about understanding how we express ourselves and act around other people.

- There are different types of social skills.

- Having good speaking skills helps you to connect with other people better.

- You can learn to speak better by reading more and listening more.

- Being funny helps you to spread happiness.

- You can learn to be funnier by sharing jokes.

- Having manners is about respecting people.

- You can learn to have better manners by teaching

others, being polite, and being kind.

The ability to communicate, understand, and respect others will boost your social confidence. Practice your social skills and become a Supergirl.

Having good social skills also includes having a secret language. If you want to know what the secret language is, I'll tell you all about it in the next chapter.

Chapter 9

9

The Secret Language That Affects Our Confidence

"The most important thing in communication is hearing what isn't said." ~ Peter F. Drucker

Hey! The secret language is called body language and is part of the fourth confidence tool. Did you know that our bodies also have a voice? It's like having a secret code that helps us understand how people are feeling without them even saying a word!

Basically, people can speak without speaking. Isn't that amazing? Like a detective on a secret mission, you're going to learn all about the incredible ways our bodies send messages to each other.

What Is Body Language, and Why Is It Important?

Body language is how our bodies speak and affects our confidence. It's a secret language that not everyone understands unless they know what body language is. So welcome to the club girlies because after you read this chapter, you'll be an expert in body language!

Body language is how we tell other people how we're thinking and feeling with our bodies; it's done without speaking. It's expressed through our hand gestures, facial expressions, and movements.

Have you ever played a game called 'charades?' If you haven't, it's a game where someone uses their body movements (a bit like sign language) to describe something like the title of a book, a TV show, or a movie. The person doing the sign language isn't allowed to speak at all, and everyone has to guess what it is. The game charades is a lot like body language.

Now, let's talk about why it's important. Well, when we speak to someone, only some things we say are expressed through our words. Even though you don't know it, most of what you say actually comes from your body language. It helps us understand how a person really feels or what they really mean, even if they don't actually say it.

For example, if your friend looks away and crosses their arms while you're telling them a story, it might mean they have something else on their mind and don't want to hear it at that moment. Or if your friend smiles a lot and nods while you're telling her a story, it shows that she's interested and wants to know more.

♥ ♥ ♥ ♥

Body language is essential because it helps us communicate better so that we can understand each other. It lets us know when a person is happy, excited, angry, or sad. Does that make sense? Here are some examples of body language:

Facial Expressions: Everyone loves using emojis to express how they're feeling. But did you know that your face is your very own emoji keyboard? I found out that there are 96 emoji facial expressions! That's a big number, right? But that's not anywhere near the number of facial expressions humans have.

Did you know that we have 43 different muscles in our faces which help us to make over 10,000 facial expressions! Can you believe that? I was so amazed when I found out this information.

So basically, humans have a secret emoji language, and when someone makes a particular expression, you know how they're feeling. Here are some examples of the facial expressions we make:

- **Happy and Sad:** When people are happy, they smile. Smiling is like sprinkling magic dust everywhere; it makes you feel great, and everyone who sees you feels great. It's like giving someone a big virtual hug! When we're sad or upset, our faces might scrunch up, and tears might trickle down our cheeks.

- **Frowns and Pouts:** When we feel down and frustrated, we might frown or pout to let other people know how we're feeling. It's like having a little rain cloud hanging over our heads. But hey, it's okay to have this expression because it lets our friends and family know how we're feeling and that we need a little bit more extra care and attention.

- **Excitement and Surprise:** Imagine opening a gift and finding it's something you've been dreaming about all year. Your face would light up with excitement and surprise, wouldn't it? When we're surprised, our eyes grow wide, and our mouths form into an 'O' shape.

- **Expressive Eyebrows:** Who knew that those caterpillar-looking things on our foreheads could say so much. But yes, they can scrunch up, wriggle, and rise to say different things. When we are surprised or confused, our eyebrows might shoot up like rockets. When we are worried about something, they might scrunch up like a piece of paper.

- **The Language of Winks:** Winks are the secret messages we send with one eye. When we wink, we are saying, "Hey, I have a secret just for you." It's a playful facial expression that can make us feel like we're part of a special club. The next time you want to share a secret, give the person a friendly wink.

The girl who is not afraid of being different

Kawaii style

Rocco

Positive Body Language

Positive body language gives people good vibes; it shows that you're feeling happy and confident. Here are some examples of positive body language:

Stand Proud and Tall: Standing tall and proud with our head held high, shoulders back, and chest out shows that we are confident and ready to take on the world.

Smile A Lot: When we smile, it's like spreading rays of sunshine to everyone we meet. A smile shows that we're approachable and friendly.

Open Arms Open Heart: Have you noticed that when someone crosses their arms in front of them, it can make them seem unapproachable like they don't want anyone to come near them? You don't want people to think that about you do you?

So instead of crossing your arms, keep them open. Open arms show that you're open to new experiences, new adventures, and open to meeting new people.

Nod, Nod, Nod: As mentioned, listening is an essential part of body language. When someone is speaking to us, we can show them that we're listening by nodding our heads. It tells them that we understand and care about what they're saying.

Making Eye Contact: It's important to make eye contact when you're speaking to someone because it shows that you're interested in what they have to say and that you're paying attention. Making eye contact also helps you connect with the person you're speaking to.

For example, when you're excited or happy, your eyes might light up or sparkle. When you're feeling sad, your eyes might have tears in them. Leonora told me a story about her experience with making eye contact, and I want her to share it with you.

Hi, girlies! I've just finished doing my English homework. I love English so much; it's one of my favorite subjects. I had to write a story about a man landing on the moon, it was really fun.

Before I started on my confidence journey, I was really shy, and I would look at the ground or look down at my feet when I was speaking to people. I didn't like making eye contact with anyone because it made me feel uncomfortable.

One day, my teacher, Mrs. Jackson, pulled me to the side and said, "Leonora, I love hearing you speak because you say so many important things, but I've noticed that you always look down when you're speaking to people, and to show how much you believe in yourself, you need to look people in the eye when you speak to them."

I felt a little bit nervous doing this, but I trusted Mrs. Jackson, and I knew that she wanted the best for me, and if I did what she said, I wouldn't be so shy anymore, so I decided to give it a try. So during recess, I went up to the new girl in my class named Gemma while she was sitting alone at the table. I took a deep breath, looked her in the eyes, and asked her if I could tell her about a new book I was reading. She said yes, and I sat down and told her all about it and kept making eye contact with her the whole way through.

Gemma's eyes were bright with excitement as I told her about the book, and that made me excited and less nervous because she was interested in what I had to say. My heart skipped with joy that day, and since then, I've been looking people in the eye every time I speak to them because I feel confident about making eye contact.

So girlies, if you're like me, and you're a bit shy and find it hard to make eye contact, do what I did. Please walk up to one of the nice kids in your class and talk to them while you're looking them in the eyes. It will give you such a massive boost of confidence that you'll always want to make eye contact when you speak to people! Making eye contact is super important and shows that you are sure of yourself.

♥ ♥ ♥ ♥ ♥

Hi, it's Marta. Leonora's story was fantastic! She's so brave, right? Do you want to be brave like Leonora? Then do everything that she tells you to do and practice, practice, practice because it will give you loads of confidence, and that's what you want, isn't it? That's great because that's what I want for you too.

Negative Body Language

The opposite of positive body language is negative body language, and you must know what it is so that you don't give people the wrong idea. Negative body language makes you look and feel less confident. Here are some examples of negative body language:

Pouts and Frowns: Negative body language can sometimes show on our faces. When we frown, pout, or look unhappy, it can make others feel sad too.

Slouching: When we hunch our shoulders or slouch, it can make us seem like we don't have any confidence and that we're not interested.

Avoiding Eye Contact: Do you remember Leonora's story? Her teacher Mrs. Jackson noticed that Leonora wasn't making eye contact when she spoke to people and told her to change it so she would look like she believed in herself.

When you don't make eye contact with the people you're speaking to, you look like you're not confident and not interested in what the person has to say.

Are you happy that you know all about the invisible language?

The next time you're speaking to a friend, watch how they move their body and see if you can hear more than what is coming out of the person's mouth.

Also, don't forget to practice good body language. So that you don't forget what you've learned in this chapter, here is a quick reminder:

- Body language is how our bodies speak; it tells people more than our words.

- Body language can include facial expressions and making eye contact.

- Facial expressions can include happy, sad, frowns, pouts, excitement, surprise, expressive eyebrows, and winks.

- Positive body language makes you feel and appear more confident.

- Negative body language makes you feel and appear less confident.

Chapter ten is the last, and it's all about the fifth and final confidence tool, which is being a force of kindness.

I know you're a kind person already, but you can learn to be extra kind, and you'll have much more confidence. How does that sound? Okay, let's see what magical treasures chapter ten has for you.

Chapter 10

10

Compassion in Action

*"If you want others to be happy, practice compassion.
If you want to be happy,
practice compassion."* ~ Dalai Lama

Hey! Are you ready to put the fifth confidence tool into action and become a force of kindness? Great, let's do this! You've probably heard the word kindness a lot. Maybe your parents or teachers have told you to be kind when you were being a little bit naughty. Kindness is a language that everyone understands, no matter what country a person comes from. When you treat a person with kindness, it gives them a warm fuzzy feeling and makes them feel fantastic. Do you want to make people feel awesome by being kind to them? Great, buckle up and get ready to dive into the magical world of kindness and what it really means.

What is Kindness?

Kindness is about caring about everyone so much that you do nice things for them even if you don't know them. Kindness is like a big magical hug for the heart. Imagine you went out shopping with your mom, and you saw a lady struggling with her bags as she was walking to her car. When you saw her, you felt bad because she was struggling, and you asked your mom if you could both go and help her. The lady was really happy for the help you gave her because it meant that her hands were not tired anymore. Kindness is about being there for people, even if you don't know them well.

Do you want to know why kindness is so great? Because it doesn't cost you anything, it's free! You don't need a lot of money to be kind; you don't need anything to be kind. Do you want to know what you need to be kind? A BIG heart! That's it. When you have a big heart, you want to make a difference in the world.

Kindness is also about treating people with respect, being a good friend, a good listener, and a good helper. Let's remember to be kind to ourselves too. Being kind to yourself means that you forgive yourself when you do something wrong, that you take care of yourself, and that you speak kindly to yourself.

Also, kindness isn't just about being kind to the people who are kind to you. It would help if you were kind to everyone at all times. I understand that you might not feel like doing this, but the world wouldn't be a very nice place if everyone was mean back to the people who were mean to them. Someone has to be the bigger person, and the bigger person can be you.

♥ ♥ ♥ ♥ ♥ ♥ ♥ ♥ ♥

How to Practice Kindness

You can make kindness a part of your personality by practicing kindness; here are some tips:

Share: When you share your stuff with other kids, it shows that you have a kind heart. It's cool to share things with your friends, but it's even cooler to share stuff with people you don't know. You can do something like give a bar of chocolate to a kid at the park the next time you go to the park with your mom.

Random Kindness: Every day, choose to do something kind for someone. It could be giving someone a compliment, helping someone in your class tie their shoelace, or washing the dishes when it's not your turn.

Include Everyone: Sometimes, the quiet kids get left out of stuff in school. They might not get picked to play sports or other games, or they don't get invited to parties because the other kids don't think they're cool enough. You can be kind to these kids by trying your best to make sure they're included in everything.

Say Kind Words: Kind words are just as magical as kindness; they spread joy and make people feel happy. Speak kind words and try your best not to say anything that will upset anyone. You can say kind words to your parents by telling them how much you appreciate them. You can compliment your friends or say something nice to someone when you pass them on the street. Use your words like magic dust and sprinkle them everywhere you go.

How Kindness Can Boost Your Confidence

Kindness is magical and fantastic because not only does it make other people feel good, but it also makes the person that's being kind feel good, and that's why it has a magical effect on your confidence. Here's how it works:

Self-Image: Practicing kindness gives you confidence. When you are kind to a person or animal and protect nature, you're making the world a better place. You feel terrific when you realize that you have something good to offer the world.

Better Friendships: Everyone loves having many friends, but strong friendships are even better. Kindness is all about caring for others and doing nice things for the people around us. Having friends that love you and want to be around you all the time makes you feel so much more confident about yourself.

It Comes Back: When you do nice things for people, others will do nice things for you without asking for it. How awesome would that make you feel?

Gives You Courage: You read earlier that you should be kind to people even if they are not kind to you. It takes a lot of courage to be able to do something like that. Let's say a kid in your class says mean things to you; you want to say mean things back, right? But guess what happens when you treat them the way they treat you? You end up not liking each other. Leonora has a wonderful story to tell about how showing kindness to someone mean gave her courage.

Hey, girlies. Okay, so do you remember I told you I used to be really shy? Well, one day, a mean girl at school called me Leona, and I decided to stay calm and ignore her. Because I ignored her, she came towards me and pulled my pigtail hard. I was really salty (upset) and ran into one of the empty classrooms, and I cried.

When I went home, I told my mom, and she said that hurt people hurt people, and what she really needs is love. So that evening, my mom helped me think of nice things I could do for the mean girl for five days. I was not too happy to do anything nice for her. I was upset because my name was Leonora, not Leona.

My mother told me not to be upset about the name-calling because Leona in English means lioness. My mother showed me a picture of the lioness. She was a beautiful female lion. Wow, I thought those animals were powerful and brave. Ok, I like the name Leona; let me try and be nice to her. This is what I did for her:

- On Monday, I gave her a lollipop

- On Tuesday, I said her hair looked nice

- On Wednesday, I told her to read a good book I had read

- On Thursday, I offered to help her with her math work

- On Friday, I gave her one of my sandwiches

On Monday the next week, she said she was sorry for pulling my hair and calling me Leona. She told me how grateful she was for being nice to her because no one was ever nice to her. We became good friends after that, and I found out that what my mom said was true, hurt people hurt people.

Even though they were mean to me, being nice to someone gave me courage because I was scared to be nice to her. What if she pulled my pigtails again? But she didn't; instead, I learned that being nice to people even when they're mean to you is the most magical thing to do because it can make a mean person turn nice. Isn't that just so awesome?

So if someone in your school is ever mean to you, try to sprinkle some magic around them, and be nice to them to see what happens. By the way, she still kept calling me Leona. We both laughed, and I loved the name.

Surround Yourself With Compassionate, Kind People Who Laugh With You

First, it's important to be around kind people because they're good to you. The last thing you want is to be around mean people because they make you feel sad and not happy, and you don't want that, do you? When someone is kind and friendly, they say nice things to you and do nice things for you. When you feel special and happy, it makes you feel more confident in being who you are.

Friends help build our Self-Confidence.

Also, you should want to be kind to other people. So when you're surrounded by kind friends, you can learn more ways to be kind to other people. Kindness is like the flu, you can catch it when you're around other kind people, and that's a good thing. When you're kind to people, they'll be kind back to you.

Now, let's talk about why it's important to be around people who you can laugh with. Do you like laughing? I do; I love it; laughing is one of my favorite things to do because it makes me feel so good. But laughing is even better when you can laugh with other people. Do you remember what it feels like to laugh so much with your friends that it makes your stomach hurt? It feels great, doesn't it? On the days that you feel sad, having friends who will make you laugh is awesome because you won't feel sad for very long. Also, it's great to laugh with people because it brings you closer together.

It's essential to surround yourself with people who think you're awesome and want to be around you because they give you confidence, accept you, support you, and they make your life fun.

♥ ♥ ♥ ♥ ♥

Let me remind you about what you've just read:

- Kindness is about caring about everyone so much that you do nice things for them even if you don't know them.

- Kindness is cool because it doesn't cost you anything.
- You can practice kindness.
- Kindness boosts your confidence.
- It's important to surround yourself with compassionate, kind people who laugh with you.

Remember to practice being kind all the time so that you become a great big shining light to everyone around you.

Conclusion

FIRST OF ALL, I want to say well done for getting to the end of the book. You're here at the conclusion, and I'm so proud of you. Throughout this book, we've explored different ways to become more confident. You now have a confidence tool kit that you can carry with you everywhere you go. Here is a quick reminder of them:

Confidence Tool #1: Get comfortable being uncomfortable - Being uncomfortable actually helps you become more confident. When you try new things or face challenges that make you feel a bit nervous, it helps you grow and learn. Maybe you're scared to speak in front of the class or try a new sport, but when you push through the discomfort, you realize you can do it! Each time you face those uncomfortable moments, you become stronger and more confident in yourself. So don't be afraid of being uncomfortable because that's how you become more confident.

Confidence Tool #2: Believe in yourself – Believing in yourself is super important. When you believe in yourself, you are confident; you know that deep down, you can do anything you set your mind to. Sometimes, things might seem hard or scary, but when you believe in yourself, you find the courage to keep going. You know that you're awesome and you can do amazing things. So don't forget to believe in yourself because you're like a shining star that can light up the whole sky!

Confidence Tool #3: Creativity – A part of being confident is being unique and having your own style. You can develop your own style by being creative and doing some of the things that Leonora told you to do. Like making your clothes look pretty by decorating them with beautiful stones, buttons, and sequins, and drawing pretty patterns on them with marker pens. Remember that everyone is creative, and you can create your own unique style when you put your mind to it.

Confidence Tool #4: Social Confidence – Having good social skills is super important. It's like having a secret code that will help you make friends and have fun when you meet new people. When you have good social skills, you are confident you can talk to people, listen to them, and understand how they're feeling. It's like having a superpower that helps you connect with others. So let's practice those skills and unlock the power of friendship and fun.

Confidence Tool #5: Be a force of kindness – Being a force of kindness means spreading love, joy, and happiness wherever you go. When you show kindness to others, you make their day brighter and fill their hearts with warmth. It can be as simple as sharing a smile, offering a helping hand, or saying kind words. You never know how much your acts of kindness can mean to someone. So let's be supergirls of kindness and make the world a better place with one act of kindness at a time!

♥ ♥ ♥ ♥ ♥

One of the most important things to remember is that confidence isn't about being perfect; it's about accepting who you are. You are unique, and that's what makes you special. When you embrace your true self, you can shine brighter than any star in the sky. Remember, you can always work on your confidence; it's like a muscle that gets stronger with practice. There might be times when you feel a little bit wobbly, and that's okay. You can always reach out to your friends for support, and you can remember that I wrote this book for you because I want you to win; we can do this together.

Please do me a favor, close your eyes, and make a promise to yourself. Promise that you're going to keep believing in yourself, keep trying new things, and keep growing and learning. When you have confidence, you can do anything! Now, I was hoping you could give me one last virtual high-five as an official member of the Confidence team! Before you go, here's a quick message from Leonora...

Hi friends, it's been so great meeting you guys, and I'm so grateful that Marta gave me this unique opportunity. I really hope that you've learned a lot from this book and that you've found your unique style, and you're learning to become more confident. I want you to remember that it takes time to develop confidence; you've got to work at it and keep practicing.

The good news is that you've got everything you need right here in this book; the only thing you've got to do is put it into action. Some days will be better than others, but on the days that you don't feel confident, just remember me. Think to yourself, if Leonora did it, I can do it too! I know I haven't met you before, but everyone who reads this book is my friend, and I keep each of you safely tucked away in my heart. I want you to pursue your dreams, stay true to who you are, and become the most confident person you can be.

KEEP SHINING.

Bye for now. *xoxoxo*

Thanks FOR READING MY BOOK!!

I hope you enjoyed this book, and that you will benefit from implementing the CONFIDENCE TOOLS that we discussed.

I would be very happy if you would take two minutes to **leave a review on Amazon.**

You will help other younger girls discover this book.

Thank you for being a part of this journey.

Your support in reading the book is very valuable to me.

Warmest regards, Marta

References

Books

Bernstein, B. (2013). *A Teen's Guide to Success: How to Be Calm, Confident, Focused*. Familius.

Downshire, J., & Grew, N. (2014). *Teenagers Translated: A Parent's Survival Guide*. Random House.

Snow, S., & Reed, Y. (2013). *Teens Have Style!: Fashion Programs for Young Adults at the Library*. ABC-CLIO.

Sokol, L., & Fox, M. (2009). *Think Confident, Be Confident: A Four-Step Program to Eliminate Doubt and Achieve Lifelong Self-Esteem*. Penguin.

Van Noord, M. (2019). *Self Help for Teens: Confidence, Assertiveness and Self-Esteem Training (3 in 1) Simple and Proven Techniques to Become Your Confident Self (for Boys and Girls)*. Help Yourself by Maria Van Noord.

Zakaria, N. (2016). *Clothing for Children and Teenagers: Anthropometry, Sizing and Fit.* Woodhead Publishing.

Websites

https://www.apparelentrepreneurship.com/how-to-create-a-fashion-mood-board/

https://yourteenmag.com/family-life/communication/ways-to-improve-communication

https://raisingchildren.net.au/pre-teens/communicating-relationships/communicating/active-listening

https://www.teenlife.com/blog/6-ways-boost-your-teens-creativity/

https://www.channelkindness.org/25-random-acts-of-kindness/#:~:text=Be%20a%20positive%20role%20model,can%20always%20be%20an%20ally.

https://raisingchildren.net.au/teens/mental-health-physical-health/about-mental-health/self-compassion-teenagers

https://www.happierhuman.com/positive-affirmations-teens/

Printed in Great Britain
by Amazon